Our courageous son, Brad

FROM

Mom & Dad

DATE

Feb 4, 2015

Proverbs 22:6

A COURAGEOUS HEART

FOR MEN

365 DAILY DEVOTIONS

Freeman-Smith, a division of Worthy Media, Inc.
134 Franklin Road, Suite 200, Brentwood, Tennessee 37027

The quoted ideas expressed in this book (but not Scripture verses) are not, in all cases, exact quotations, as some have been edited for clarity and brevity. In all cases, the author has attempted to maintain the speaker's original intent. In some cases, quoted material for this book was obtained from secondary sources, primarily print media. While every effort was made to ensure the accuracy of these sources, the accuracy cannot be guaranteed. For additions, deletions, corrections, or clarifications in future editions of this text, please write Freeman-Smith.

Cover Design by Kim Russell / Wahoo Designs
Page Layout by Bart Dawson

ISBN 978-1-60587-452-4

Printed in the United States of America

3 4 5—CHG—17 16 15 14

A COURAGEOUS HEART

FOR MEN

365 DAILY DEVOTIONS

INTRODUCTION

How desperately our world needs courageous Christian men who are willing to honor God with their prayers and their service! This generation faces problems that defy easy solutions, yet face them we must. So we need leaders whose vision is clear and whose intentions are pure.

Daniel observed, "Those who are wise will shine like the brightness of the heavens, and those who lead many to righteousness, like the stars for ever and ever" (12:3 NIV). Hopefully, you are determined to become such a man—a man who shares his wisdom and his courage with family, friends, and co-workers.

In your hands, you hold a book that contains 365 devotional readings. These readings contain Bible verses, brief essays, and inspirational quotations from noted Christian thinkers. During the next 365 days, please try this experiment: read a page from this book each day. If you're already committed to a daily time of worship, this book will enrich that experience. If you are not, the simple act of giving God a few minutes each morning will change the direction and the quality of your life.

Each day provides opportunities for all of us to put God where He belongs: at the center of our lives. When we do so, we worship Him, not just with words, but with deeds. And, we become dutiful servants of God, courageous men who share His Son's message of love and salvation with the world.

May you be such a man—and may you share your courage and your wisdom with a world that needs both.

BEING A MAN OF PRAYER

Rejoice always, pray without ceasing, in everything give thanks; for this is the will of God in Christ Jesus for you.

1 Thessalonians 5:16-18 NKJV

Is prayer an integral part of your daily life, or is it a hit-or-miss habit? Do you "pray without ceasing," or is your prayer life an afterthought? Do you regularly pray in the solitude of the early morning darkness, or do you lower your head only when others are watching? The answer to these questions will determine the direction of your day—and your life.

So here's your challenge: make yourself a man of prayer. Begin your prayers early in the morning and continue them throughout the day. And remember this: God does answer your prayers, but He's not likely to answer those prayers until you've prayed them.

Prayer is the most important tool for your mission to the world. People may refuse our love or reject our message, but they are defenseless against our prayers.

Rick Warren

NEED COURAGE? GOD CAN HANDLE IT

Do not be afraid or discouraged, for the LORD is the one who goes before you. He will be with you; he will neither fail you nor forsake you.

Deuteronomy 31:8 NLT

Life can be difficult and discouraging at times. During our darkest moments, God offers us courage and strength if we turn our hearts and our prayers to Him.

As believing Christians, we have every reason to live courageously. After all, the ultimate battle has already been fought and won on the cross at Calvary. But sometimes, because we are imperfect human beings who possess imperfect faith, we fall prey to fear and doubt. The answer to our fears, of course, is God.

The next time you find your courage tested to the limit, remember that God is as near as your next breath. He is your shield and your strength; He is your protector and your deliverer. Call upon Him in your hour of need and then be comforted. Whatever your challenge, whatever your trouble, God can handle it . . . and will!

USING YOUR GIFTS

God has given gifts to each of you from his great variety of spiritual gifts. Manage them well so that God's generosity can flow through you.

1 Peter 4:10 NLT

All men possess special gifts—bestowed from the Father above—and you are no exception. But, your gift is no guarantee of success; it must be cultivated and nurtured; otherwise, it will go unused . . . and God's gift to you will be squandered.

Today, make a promise to yourself that you will earnestly seek to discover the talents that God has given you. Then, nourish those talents and make them grow. Finally, vow to share your gifts with the world for as long as God gives you the power to do so. After all, the best way to say "Thank You" for God's gifts is to use them.

One thing taught large in the Holy Scriptures is that while God gives His gifts freely, He will require a strict accounting of them at the end of the road.

A. W. Tozer

BLESSED THROUGH OBEDIENCE

By this we know that we have come to know Him, if we keep His commandments.

1 John 2:3 NASB

God gave us His commandments for a reason: so that we might obey them and be blessed. Oswald Chambers, the author of the Christian classic devotional text, *My Utmost for His Highest*, advised, "Never support an experience which does not have God as its source, and faith in God as its result." These words serve as a powerful reminder that, as Christians, we are called to walk with God and obey His commandments. But, we live in a world that presents us with countless temptations to stray far from God's path. We Christians, when confronted with sin, have clear instructions: Walk—or better yet run—in the opposite direction.

If men will not be governed by the Ten Commandments, they shall be governed by the ten thousand commandments.

G. K. Chesterton

Love the knowledge of the Scriptures and you will not love the errors of the flesh.

St. Jerome

ENDLESS POSSIBILITIES

Is anything too hard for the L*ORD?*

Genesis 18:14 KJV

Ours is a God of infinite possibilities. But sometimes, because of limited faith and limited understanding, we wrongly assume that God cannot or will not intervene in the affairs of mankind. Such assumptions are simply wrong.

Are you afraid to ask God to do big things in your life? Is your faith threadbare and worn? If so, it's time to abandon your doubts and reclaim your faith in God's promises.

God's Holy Word makes it clear: absolutely nothing is impossible for the Lord. And since the Bible means what it says, you can be comforted in the knowledge that the Creator of the universe can do miraculous things in your own life and in the lives of your loved ones. Your challenge, as a believer, is to take God at His word, and to expect the miraculous.

So God's patience is His power over Himself. Great is that God who, having all power, yet keeps all power subject to Himself.

Jim Elliot

DEPENDING ON GOD

Therefore humble yourselves under the mighty hand of God, that He may exalt you at the proper time, casting all your anxiety on Him, because He cares for you.

1 Peter 5:6-7 NASB

God is a never-ending source of support and courage for those of us who call upon Him. When we are weary, He gives us strength. When we see no hope, God reminds us of His promises. When we grieve, God wipes away our tears.

Do the demands of this day threaten to overwhelm you? If so, you must rely not only upon your own resources but also upon the promises of your Father in heaven. God will hold your hand and walk with you every day of your life if you let Him. So even if your circumstances are difficult, trust the Father. His love is eternal and His goodness endures forever.

Faith is not merely you holding on to God—it is God holding on to you.

E. Stanley Jones

Jesus does not say, "There is no storm." He says, I am here, do not toss, but trust."

Vance Havner

GROWING IN CHRIST

When I was a child, I spoke as a child, I understood as a child, I thought as a child; but when I became a man, I put away childish things.

1 Corinthians 13:11 NKJV

God doesn't intend for any of us to be stagnate. Far from it! God's plan for us includes a lifetime of personal and spiritual growth—a lifetime of learning from our experiences . . . and sharing what we've learned.

We can and should continue to grow throughout every stage of life. But if we cease to grow, either emotionally or spiritually, we do ourselves and our loved ones a profound disservice.

It's a familiar saying, and it's true: "You aren't getting older, you're getting better!" And it's up to you to keep getting better every day that you live. When you do, you'll continue to shine your light upon a world that needs all the maturity and wisdom it can get.

Every great company, every great brand, and every great career has been built in exactly the same way: bit by bit, step by step, little by little.

John Maxwell

HONORING GOD

Honor GOD with everything you own; give him the first and the best. Your barns will burst, your wine vats will brim over.

Proverbs 3:9-10 MSG

Whom will you choose to honor today? If you honor God and place Him at the center of your life, every day is a cause for celebration. But if you fail to honor your Heavenly Father, you're asking for trouble, and lots of it.

At times, your life is probably hectic, demanding, and complicated. When the demands of life leave you rushing from place to place with scarcely a moment to spare, you may fail to pause and thank your Creator for the blessings He has bestowed upon you. But that's a big mistake. So honor God for who He is and for what He has done for you. And don't just honor Him on Sunday morning. Praise Him all day long, every day, for as long as you live . . . and then for all eternity.

We should be so consumed with God's glory that we hurt when He is dishonored.

John MacArthur

THE POWER OF YOUR WORDS

From a wise mind comes wise speech; the words of the wise are persuasive.

Proverbs 16:23 NLT

God's Word reminds us that "Reckless words pierce like a sword, but the tongue of the wise brings healing" (Proverbs 12:18 NIV). If you seek to be a source of encouragement to friends, to family members, and to co-workers, then you must measure your words carefully. And that's exactly what God wants you to do.

Today, make this promise to yourself: vow to be an honest, effective, encouraging communicator at work, at home, and every place in between. Speak wisely, not impulsively. Use words of kindness and praise, not words of anger or derision. Learn how to be truthful without being cruel. Remember that you have the power to heal others or to injure them, to lift others up or to hold them back. And when you learn how to lift them up, you'll soon discover that you've lifted yourself up, too.

Attitude and the spirit in which we communicate are as important as the words we say.

Charles Stanley

THE STORMS OF LIFE

But Jesus immediately said to them: "Take courage! It is I. Don't be afraid."

Matthew 14:27 NIV

A storm rose quickly on the Sea of Galilee, and the disciples were afraid. Although they had seen Jesus perform many miracles, the disciples feared for their lives, so they turned to their Savior, and He calmed the waters and the wind.

Sometimes, we, like the disciples, feel threatened by the inevitable storms of life. And when we are fearful, we, too, can turn to Christ for courage and for comfort.

The next time you're afraid, remember that the One who calmed the wind and the waves is also your personal Savior. And remember that the ultimate battle has already been won at Calvary. We, as believers, can live courageously in the promises of our Lord . . . and we should.

Down through the centuries, in times of trouble and trial, God has brought courage to the hearts of those who love Him. The Bible is filled with assurances of God's help and comfort in every kind of trouble.

Billy Graham

AT PEACE WITH YOUR PURPOSE

But now in Christ Jesus you who once were far off have been brought near by the blood of Christ. For He Himself is our peace.

Ephesians 2:13-14 NKJV

Are you at peace with the direction of your life? If you're a Christian, you should be. Perhaps you seek a new direction or a sense of renewed purpose, but those feelings should never rob you of the genuine peace that can and should be yours through a personal relationship with Jesus.

Have you found the lasting peace that can be yours through Jesus, or are you still rushing after the illusion of "peace and happiness" that our world promises but cannot deliver? Today, as a gift to yourself, to your family, and to your friends, claim the inner peace that is your spiritual birthright: the peace of Jesus Christ.

That peace, which has been described and which believers enjoy, is a participation of the peace which their glorious Lord and Master himself enjoys.

Jonathan Edwards

THE IMPORTANCE OF PRAYER

Be anxious for nothing, but in everything by prayer and supplication, with thanksgiving, let your requests be made known to God.

Philippians 4:6 NKJV

Prayer is a powerful tool for communicating with our Creator; it is an opportunity to commune with the Giver of all things good. Prayer is not a thing to be taken lightly or to be used infrequently. Prayer should never be reserved for mealtimes or for bedtimes; it should be an ever-present focus in our daily lives.

In his first letter to the Thessalonians, Paul wrote, "Rejoice evermore. Pray without ceasing. In every thing give thanks: for this is the will of God in Christ Jesus concerning you" (5:17-18 KJV). Paul's words apply to every Christian of every generation. So, let us pray constantly about things great and small. God is listening, and He wants to hear from us. Now.

If you lack knowledge, go to school. If you lack wisdom, get on your knees.

Vance Havner

LIVING RIGHTEOUSLY

Run away from infantile indulgence. Run after mature righteousness—faith, love, peace—joining those who are in honest and serious prayer before God.

2 *Timothy* 2:22 MSG

A life of righteousness is lived in accordance with God's commandments. A righteous man strives to be faithful, honest, generous, disciplined, loving, kind, humble, and grateful, to name only a few of the more obvious qualities which are described in God's Word.

If we seek to follow the steps of Jesus, we must seek to live according to His teachings. In short, we must, to the best of our abilities, live according to the principles contained in the Holy Bible. When we do, we become powerful examples to our families and friends of the blessings that God bestows upon righteous men.

We must appropriate the tender mercy of God every day after conversion, or problems quickly develop. We need his grace daily in order to live a righteous life.

Jim Cymbala

SHARING THE WEALTH

If you give, you will receive. Your gift will return to you in full measure, pressed down, shaken together to make room for more, and running over. Whatever measure you use in giving—large or small—it will be used to measure what is given back to you.

Luke 6:38 NLT

Are you anxious to share the gifts that God has given you, or are you inclined to do otherwise? The Bible makes it clear that Christ came to this earth so that His followers might enjoy His abundance (John 10:10). But what, exactly, did Jesus mean when He promised "life . . . more abundantly"? Was He referring to material possessions or financial wealth? Hardly. Jesus offers a different kind of abundance: a spiritual richness that extends beyond the temporal boundaries of this world.

Is material abundance part of God's plan for our lives? Perhaps. But in every circumstance of life, during times of wealth or times of want, God will provide us what we need if we trust Him (Matthew 6). May we, as believers, claim God's riches (in whatever form they may appear), and may we share those blessings with all who cross our path.

ONE MOUTH, TWO EARS

Everyone should be quick to listen, slow to speak and slow to become angry, for man's anger does not bring about the righteous life that God desires.

James 1:19-20 NIV

Perhaps God gave each of us one mouth and two ears in order that we might listen twice as much as we speak. Unfortunately, many of us do otherwise, especially when we become angry.

Anger is a natural human emotion that is sometimes necessary and appropriate. Even Jesus Himself became angered when He confronted the moneychangers in the temple. But, more often than not, our frustrations are of the more mundane variety. When you are tempted to lose your temper over the minor inconveniences of life, don't. Turn away from anger, and turn instead to God.

Fill the heart with the love of Christ so that only truth and purity can come out of the mouth.

Warren Wiersbe

The great test of a man's character is his tongue.

Oswald Chambers

HE WANTS YOU TO ASK

He granted their request because they trusted in Him.

1 Chronicles 5:20 HCSB

Sometimes, amid the demands and the frustrations of everyday life, we forget to slow ourselves down long enough to talk with God. Instead of turning our thoughts and prayers to Him, we rely upon our own resources. Instead of praying for strength and courage, we seek to manufacture it within ourselves. Instead of asking God for guidance, we depend only upon our own limited wisdom. The results of such behaviors are unfortunate and, on occasion, tragic.

Are you in need? Ask God to sustain you. Are you troubled? Take your worries to Him in prayer. Are you weary? Seek God's strength. In all things great and small, seek God's wisdom and His grace. He hears your prayers, and He will answer. All you must do is ask.

There is a communion with God that asks for nothing, yet asks for everything . . . He who seeks the Father more than anything he can give is likely to have what he asks, for he is not likely to ask amiss.

George MacDonald

A BOOK UNLIKE ANY OTHER

For I am not ashamed of the gospel, because it is God's power for salvation to everyone who believes.

Romans 1:16 HCSB

God's Word is unlike any other book. A. W. Tozer wrote, "The purpose of the Bible is to bring men to Christ, to make them holy and prepare them for heaven. In this it is unique among books, and it always fulfills its purpose." As Christians, we are called upon to study God's Holy Word and then to share it with the world.

The Bible is a priceless gift, a tool for Christians to use as they share the Good News of their Savior, Christ Jesus. Too many Christians, however, keep their spiritual tool kits tightly closed and out of sight. Jonathan Edwards advised, "Be assiduous in reading the Holy Scriptures. This is the fountain whence all knowledge in divinity must be derived. Therefore let not this treasure lie by you neglected." God's Holy Word is, indeed, a priceless, one-of-a-kind treasure. Handle it with care, but, more importantly, handle it every day.

The vigor of our spiritual lives will be in exact proportion to the place held by the Bible in our lives and in our thoughts.

George Mueller

ACKNOWLEDGING YOUR BLESSINGS

The L*ORD bless you and keep you; The* L*ORD make His face shine upon you, And be gracious to you.*

Numbers 6:24-25 NKJV

When the demands of life leave us rushing from place to place with scarcely a moment to spare, we may fail to pause and thank our Creator for His gifts. But, whenever we neglect to give proper thanks to the Father, we suffer because of our misplaced priorities.

Today, begin making a list of your blessings. You most certainly will not be able to make a complete list, but take a few moments and jot down as many blessings as you can. Then, give thanks to the Giver of all good things: God. His love for you is eternal, as are His gifts. And it's never too soon—or too late—to offer Him thanks.

God's kindness is not like the sunset—brilliant in its intensity, but dying every second. God's generosity keeps coming and coming and coming.

Bill Hybels

MID-COURSE CORRECTIONS

The prudent see danger and take refuge, but the simple keep going and suffer from it.

Proverbs 27:12 NIV

In our fast-paced world, everyday life has become an exercise in managing change. Our circumstances change; our relationships change; our bodies change. We grow older every day, as does our world. Thankfully, God does not change. He is eternal, as are the truths that are found in His Holy Word.

Are you facing one of life's inevitable "mid-course corrections"? If so, you must place your faith, your trust, and your life in the hands of the One who does not change: your Heavenly Father. He is the unmoving rock upon which you must construct this day and every day. When you do, you are secure.

Sometimes your medicine bottle says, "Shake well before using." That is what God has to do with some of his people. He has to shake them well before they are usable.

Vance Havner

CHOOSING RIGHTEOUSNESS

I am offering you life or death, blessings or curses. Now, choose life! . . . To choose life is to love the L*ORD your God, obey him, and stay close to him.*

Deuteronomy 30:19-20 NCV

Sometimes, because you're an imperfect human being, you may become so wrapped up in meeting society's expectations that you fail to focus on God's expectations. To do so is a mistake of major proportions—don't make it. Instead, seek God's guidance as you focus your energies on becoming the best "you" that you can possibly be. And, when it comes to matters of conscience, seek approval not from your peers, but from your Creator.

Whom will you try to please today: God or man? Your primary obligation is not to please imperfect men and women. Your obligation is to strive diligently to meet the expectations of an all-knowing and perfect God. Trust Him always. Love Him always. Praise Him always. And make choices that please Him. Always.

The greatest choice any man makes is to let God choose for him.

Vance Havner

HUMBLED BY HIS SACRIFICE

But as for me, I will never boast about anything except the cross of our Lord Jesus Christ, through whom the world has been crucified to me, and I to the world.

Galatians 6:14 HCSB

As we consider Christ's sacrifice on the cross, we should be profoundly humbled. And today, as we come to Christ in prayer, we should do so in a spirit of humble devotion.

Christ humbled Himself on a cross—for you. He shed His blood—for you. He has offered to walk with you through this life and throughout all eternity. As you approach Him today in prayer, think about His sacrifice and His grace. And be humble.

The infinite value of each human soul is not a Christian doctrine. God did not die for man because of some value He perceived in him. The value of each human soul considered simply in itself, out of relation to God, is zero. As St. Paul writes, to have died for valuable men would have been not divine, but merely heroic; but God died for sinners. He loved us not because we were lovable, but because He is Love.

C. S. *Lewis*

GOD'S ASSURANCE

I've told you all this so that trusting me, you will be unshakable and assured, deeply at peace. In this godless world you will continue to experience difficulties. But take heart! I've conquered the world.

John 16:33 MSG

Are you a confident believer, or do you live under a cloud of uncertainty and doubt? As a Christian, you have many reasons to be confident. After all, God is in His heaven; Christ has risen; and you are the recipient of God's grace. Despite these blessings, you may, from time to time, find yourself being tormented by negative emotions—and you are certainly not alone.

Even the most faithful Christians are overcome by occasional bouts of fear and doubt. You are no different.

But even when you feel very distant from God, remember that God is never distant from you. When you sincerely seek His presence, He will touch your heart, calm your fears, and restore your confidence.

At least ten times every day, affirm this thought: "I expect the best and, with God's help, will attain the best."

Norman Vincent Peale

HOPE FOR THE JOURNEY

Since God assured us, "I'll never let you down, never walk off and leave you," we can boldly quote, God is there, ready to help; I'm fearless no matter what.

Hebrews 13:5-6 MSG

Because we are saved by a risen Christ, we can have hope for the future, no matter how desperate our circumstances may seem. After all, God has promised that we are His throughout eternity. And, He has told us that we must place our hopes in Him.

Today, summon the courage to follow God. Even if the path seems difficult, even if your heart is fearful, trust your Heavenly Father and follow Him. Trust Him with your day and your life. Do His work, care for His children, and share His Good News. Let Him guide your steps. He will not lead you astray.

Many things are possible for the person who has hope. Even more is possible for the person who has faith. And still more is possible for the person who knows how to love. But everything is possible for the person who practices all three virtues.

Brother Lawrence

DURING DARK DAYS

I have heard your prayer, I have seen your tears; surely I will heal you.

2 Kings 20:5 NKJV

The sadness that accompanies any significant loss is an inevitable fact of life. In time, sadness runs its course and gradually abates. Depression, on the other hand, is a physical and emotional condition that is highly treatable.

If you find yourself feeling "blue," perhaps it's a logical reaction to the ups and downs of daily life. But if you or someone close to you have become dangerously depressed, it's time to seek professional help.

Some days are light and happy, and some days are not. When we face the inevitable dark days of life, we must choose how we will respond. Will we allow ourselves to sink even more deeply into our own sadness, or will we do the difficult work of pulling ourselves out? We bring light to the dark days of life by turning first to God, and then to trusted family members, friends, and medical professionals. When we do, the clouds will eventually part, and the sun will shine once more upon our souls.

A WORTHY DISCIPLE

He has showed you, O man, what is good. And what does the L*ORD* *require of you? To act justly and to love mercy and to walk humbly with your God.*

Micah 6:8 NIV

The twelve disciples came from all different walks of life: blue collar and professionals, including fishermen and a tax collector. They were from different political spectrums, including some passionate zealots. These twelve men came with diverse personalities and emotional traits: from Peter the impulsive to Thomas the doubter.

God is still in the business of acquiring disciples: ditch diggers and presidents; Republicans, Democrats, and independents; introverts and extroverts. His only criterion is that you believe in Him and be willing to sacrifice your all for His kingdom's work.

Real men become disciples by forsaking all and giving their lives to Christ. It is not easy, but those who stay the course are rewarded with a life of passion and purpose.

Discipleship is a daily discipline: we follow Jesus a step at a time, a day at a time.

Warren Wiersbe

THE SON OF ENCOURAGEMENT

A cheerful look brings joy to the heart, and good news gives health to the bones.

Proverbs 15:30 NIV

Barnabas, a man whose name meant "Son of Encouragement," was a leader in the early Christian church. He was known for his kindness and for his ability to encourage others. Because of Barnabas, many people were introduced to Christ. And today, as believers living in a difficult world, we must seek to imitate the "Son of Encouragement."

We imitate Barnabas when we speak kind words to our families and to our friends. We imitate Barnabas when our actions give credence to our beliefs. We imitate Barnabas when we are generous with our possessions and with our praise. We imitate Barnabas when we give hope to the hopeless and encouragement to the downtrodden.

Today, be like Barnabas: become a source of encouragement to those who cross your path. When you do so, you will quite literally change the world, one person—and one moment—at a time.

GOD'S ALLY

Be self-controlled and alert. Your enemy the devil prowls around like a roaring lion looking for someone to devour. Resist him, standing firm in the faith . . . .

1 Peter 5:8-9 NIV

Nineteenth-century clergyman Edwin Hubbel Chapin warned, "Neutral men are the devil's allies." His words were true then, and they're true now. Neutrality in the face of evil is a sin. Yet all too often, we fail to fight evil, not because we are neutral, but because we are shortsighted: we don't fight the devil because we don't recognize his handiwork.

If we are to recognize evil and fight it, we must pay careful attention. We must pay attention to God's Word, and we must pay attention to the realities of everyday life. When we observe life objectively, and when we do so with eyes and hearts that are attuned to God's Holy Word, we can no longer be neutral believers. And when we are no longer neutral, God rejoices while the devil despairs.

The only thing necessary for the triumph of evil is for good men to do nothing.

Edmund Burke

MOUNTAIN-MOVING FAITH

But someone may well say, "You have faith and I have works; show me your faith without the works, and I will show you my faith by my works."

James 2:18 NASB

It is important to remember that the work required to build and sustain our faith is an ongoing process. Corrie ten Boom advised, "Be filled with the Holy Spirit; join a church where the members believe the Bible and know the Lord; seek the fellowship of other Christians; learn and be nourished by God's Word and His many promises. Conversion is not the end of your journey—it is only the beginning."

The work of nourishing your faith can and should be joyful work. The hours that you invest in Bible study, prayer, meditation, and worship should be times of enrichment and celebration. And, as you continue to build your life upon a foundation of faith, you will discover that the journey toward spiritual maturity lasts a lifetime. As a child of God, you are never fully "grown": instead, you can continue "growing up" every day of your life. And that's exactly what God wants you to do.

FINANCIAL SECURITY

Honor the Lord with your wealth and the firstfruits from all your crops. Then your barns will be full, and your wine barrels will overflow with new wine.

Proverbs 3:9-10 NCV

The quest for financial security is a journey that leads us across many peaks and through a few unexpected valleys. When we reach the mountaintops, we find it easy to praise God and to give thanks. But, when we face disappointment or financial hardship, it seems so much more difficult to trust God's perfect plan. But, trust Him we must.

As you strive to achieve financial security for your family, remember this: The next time you find your courage tested to the limit (and it will be), lean upon God's promises. Trust His Son. Remember that God is always near and that He is your protector and your deliverer. Always.

One of the dangers of having a lot of money is that you may be quite satisfied with the kinds of happiness money can give and so fail to realize your need for God. If everything seems to come simply by signing checks, you may forget that you are at every moment totally dependent on God.

C. S. Lewis

NOW IS THE TIME

So, my son, throw yourself into this work for Christ.

2 Timothy 1:1 MSG

God's love for you is deeper and more profound than you can imagine. God's love for you is so great that He sent His only Son to this earth to die for your sins and to offer you the priceless gift of eternal life. Now, you must decide whether or not to accept God's gift. Will you ignore it or embrace it? Will you return it or neglect it? Will you accept Christ's love and build a lifelong relationship with Him, or will you turn away from Him and take a different path?

Your decision to allow Christ to reign over your heart is the pivotal decision of your life. It is a decision that you cannot ignore. It is a decision that is yours and yours alone. Accept God's gift now: allow His Son to preside over your heart, your thoughts, and your life, starting this instant.

If we seek salvation, we are taught by the very name of Jesus that it is "of him." If we seek any other gifts of the Spirit, they will be found in his anointing. If we seek strength, it lies in his dominion; if purity, in his conception; if gentleness, it appears in his birth.

John Calvin

A LIFE OF FULFILLMENT

For You, O God, have tested us; You have refined us as silver is refined . . . we went through fire and through water; but You brought us out to rich fulfillment.

Psalm 66:10-12 NKJV

Everywhere we turn, or so it seems, the world promises fulfillment, contentment, and happiness. But the contentment that the world offers is fleeting and incomplete. Thankfully, the fulfillment that God offers is all encompassing and everlasting.

Sometimes, amid the inevitable hustle and bustle of life here on earth, we can forfeit—albeit temporarily—the joy of Christ as we wrestle with the challenges of daily living. Yet God's Word is clear: fulfillment through Christ is available to all who seek it and claim it. Count yourself among that number. Seek first a personal, transforming relationship with Jesus, and then claim the joy, the fulfillment, and the spiritual abundance that the Shepherd offers His sheep.

Find satisfaction in him who made you, and only then find satisfaction in yourself as part of his creation.

St. Augustine

GOD IS LOVE

God is love; and he that dwelleth in love dwelleth in God, and God in him.

1 John 4:16 KJV

The Bible makes this promise: God is love. It's a sweeping statement, a profoundly important description of what God is and how God works. God's love is perfect. When we open our hearts to His perfect love, we are touched by the Creator's hand, and we are transformed.

Today, even if you can only carve out a few quiet moments, offer sincere prayers of thanksgiving to your Creator. He loves you now and throughout all eternity. Open your heart to His presence and His love.

The life of faith is a daily exploration of the constant and countless ways in which God's grace and love are experienced.

Eugene Peterson

As we stand at the Cross of Christ, we see a glorious exhibition of God's love.

Billy Graham

WHY HE SENT HIS SON

For all have sinned and fall short of the glory of God, and are justified freely by his grace through the redemption that came by Christ Jesus.

Romans 3:23-24 NIV

Despite our shortcomings, God sent His Son so that we might be redeemed from our sins. In doing so, our Heavenly Father demonstrated His infinite mercy and His infinite love. We have received countless gifts from God, but none can compare with the gift of salvation. God's grace is the ultimate gift, and we owe Him the ultimate in thanksgiving.

Christ sacrificed His life on the cross so that we might have eternal life. This gift, freely given from God's only begotten Son, is the priceless possession of everyone who accepts Him as Lord and Savior. We return our Savior's love by welcoming Him into our hearts and sharing His message and His love. When we do so, we are blessed here on earth and throughout all eternity.

All men who live with any degree of serenity live by some assurance of grace.

Reinhold Niebuhr

STRENGTH FOR THE DAY

I can do all things through Christ which strengtheneth me.

Philippians 4:13 KJV

Have you made God the cornerstone of your life, or is He relegated to a few hours on Sunday morning? Have you genuinely allowed God to reign over every corner of your heart, or have you attempted to place Him in a spiritual compartment? The answer to these questions will determine the direction of your day and your life.

God loves you. In times of trouble, He will comfort you; in times of sorrow, He will dry your tears. When you are weak or sorrowful, God is as near as your next breath. He stands at the door of your heart and waits. Welcome Him in and allow Him to rule. And then, accept the peace, the strength, the protection, and the abundance that only God can give.

God is great and God is powerful, but we must invite him to be powerful in our lives. His strength is always there, but it's up to us to provide a channel through which that power can flow.

Bill Hybels

A SACRIFICIAL LOVE

I am the good shepherd. The good shepherd lays down his life for the sheep.

John 10:11 NIV

How much does Christ love us? More than we, as mere mortals, can comprehend. His love is perfect and steadfast. Even though we are fallible and wayward, the Shepherd cares for us still. Even though we have fallen far short of the Father's commandments, Christ loves us with a power and depth that is beyond our understanding. The sacrifice that Jesus made upon the cross was made for each of us, and His love endures to the edge of eternity and beyond.

Christ's love changes everything. When you accept His gift of grace, you are transformed, not only for today, but also for all eternity. If you haven't already done so, accept Jesus Christ as your Savior. He's waiting patiently for you to invite Him into your heart. Please don't make Him wait a single minute longer.

It was not for societies or states that Christ died, but for men.

C. S. Lewis

A CLEAR CONSCIENCE

If then you were raised with Christ, seek those things which are above, where Christ is, sitting at the right hand of God. Set your mind on things above, not on things on the earth.

Colossians 3:1-2 NKJV

Few things in life torment us more than a guilty conscience. And, few things in life provide more contentment than the knowledge that we are obeying God's commandments.

A clear conscience is one of the rewards we earn when we obey God's Word and follow His will. When we follow God's will and accept His gift of salvation, our earthly rewards are never-ceasing, and our heavenly rewards are everlasting.

Christian joy is a gift from God flowing from a good conscience.

St. Philip Neri

Guilt is a gift that leads us to grace.

Franklin Graham

CONSIDERING THE CROSS

But God forbid that I should boast except in the cross of our Lord Jesus Christ, by whom the world has been crucified to me, and I to the world.

Galatians 6:14 NKJV

As we consider Christ's sacrifice on the cross, we should be profoundly humbled and profoundly grateful. And today, as we come to Christ in prayer, we should do so in a spirit of quiet, heartfelt devotion to the One who gave His life so that we might have life eternal.

He was the Son of God, but He wore a crown of thorns. He was the Savior of mankind, yet He was put to death on a roughhewn cross made of wood. He offered His healing touch to an unsaved world, and yet the same hands that had healed the sick and raised the dead were pierced with nails.

Christ humbled Himself on a cross—for you. As you approach Him today in prayer, think about His love and His sacrifice. And be grateful.

On a hill far away stood an old rugged cross, the emblem of suffering and shame; and I love that old cross where the dearest and best for a world of lost sinners was slain.

George Bennard

ENTHUSIASTIC DISCIPLESHIP

Do your work with enthusiasm. Work as if you were serving the Lord, not as if you were serving only men and women.

Ephesians 6:7 NCV

With whom will you choose to walk today? Will you walk with shortsighted people who honor the ways of the world, or will you walk with the Son of God? Jesus walks with you. Are you walking with Him? Hopefully, you will choose to walk with Him today and every day of your life.

Jesus has called upon believers of every generation (and that includes you) to follow in His footsteps. And God's Word promises that when you follow in Christ's footsteps, you will learn how to live freely and lightly (Matthew 11:28-30).

Jesus doesn't want you to be a run-of-the-mill, follow-the-crowd kind of person. Jesus wants you to be a "new creation" through Him. And that's exactly what you should want for yourself, too. Jesus deserves your extreme enthusiasm; the world deserves it; and you deserve the experience of sharing it.

THE POWER OF WORDS

Watch the way you talk. Let nothing foul or dirty come out of your mouth. Say only what helps, each word a gift.

Ephesians 4:29 MSG

The words that we speak have the power to do great good or great harm. If we speak words of encouragement and hope, we can lift others up. And that's exactly what God commands us to do!

Sometimes, when we feel uplifted and secure, it is easy to speak kind words. Other times, when we are discouraged or tired, we can scarcely summon the energy to uplift ourselves, much less anyone else. God intends that we speak words of kindness, wisdom, and truth, no matter our circumstances, no matter our emotions. When we do, we share a priceless gift with the world, and we give glory to the One who gave His life for us. As believers, we must do no less.

The truest help we can render an afflicted man is not to take his burden from him, but to call out his best energy, that he may be able to bear the burden himself.

Phillips Brooks

A PASSION FOR LIFE

Those who hope in the Lord *will renew their strength. They will soar on wings like eagles; they will run and not grow weary, they will walk and not be faint.*

Isaiah 40:31 NIV

Are you "burning" with enthusiasm about your life, your friends, your family, and your future? If so, congratulations, and keep up the good work! But, if your spiritual batteries are running low, perhaps you're spending too much energy focusing on your losses and too little time planning for future victories.

Writer Sara Jordan has this simple (but effective) advice: "Every day give yourself a good mental shampoo."

So if you're feeling tired, or troubled, or both, don't despair. Instead, take time to count your blessings as you focus on things positive. And while you're at it, seek strength from the Source that never fails. When you sincerely petition God, He will give you all the strength you need to live victoriously through Him.

Christianity, if false, is of no importance, and, if true, of infinite importance. The one thing it cannot be is moderately important.

C. S. Lewis

TEMPORARY SETBACKS

A time to weep, and a time to laugh; a time to mourn, and a time to dance . . . .

Ecclesiastes 3:4 KJV

The occasional disappointments and failures of life are inevitable. Such setbacks are simply the price that we must occasionally pay for our willingness to take risks as we follow our dreams. But even when we encounter bitter disappointments, we must never lose faith.

When we encounter the inevitable difficulties of life here on earth, God stands ready to protect us. Our responsibility, of course, is to ask Him for protection. When we call upon Him in heartfelt prayer, He will answer—in His own time and according to His own plan—and He will heal us. And, while we are waiting for God's plans to unfold and for His healing touch to restore us, we can be comforted in the knowledge that our Creator can overcome any obstacle, even if we cannot.

Goals are worth setting and worth missing. We learn from nonsuccesses.

Bill Bright

AN AWESOME GOD

The fear of the L*ORD* *is a fountain of life . . . .*

Proverbs 14:27 NIV

Do you have a healthy, fearful respect for God's power? If so, you are both wise and obedient. And, because you are a thoughtful believer, you also understand that genuine wisdom begins with a profound appreciation for God's limitless power.

God praises humility and punishes pride. That's why God's greatest servants will always be those humble men and women who care less for their own glory and more for God's glory. In God's kingdom, the only way to achieve greatness is to shun it. And the only way to be wise is to understand these facts: God is great; He is all-knowing; and He is all-powerful. We must respect Him, and we must humbly obey His commandments, or we must accept the consequences of our misplaced pride.

When true believers are awed by the greatness of God and by the privilege of becoming His children, then they become sincerely motivated, effective evangelists.

Bill Hybels

RECOUPING YOUR LOSSES

Misfortune pursues the sinner, but prosperity is the reward of the righteous.

Proverbs 13:21 NIV

Have you ever made a financial blunder? If so, welcome to a very large club! Almost everyone experiences financial pressures from time to time, and so, perhaps, will you.

When we commit the inevitable missteps of life, we must correct them, learn from them, and pray for the wisdom not to repeat them. When we do, our mistakes become lessons, and our lives become adventures in growth, not stagnation.

So here's the big question: Have you used your mistakes as stumbling blocks or stepping stones? The answer to that question will determine how quickly you gain financial security and peace of mind.

Christians cannot experience peace in the area of finances until they have surrendered total control of this area to God and accepted their position as stewards.

Larry Burkett

LOVE THAT FORGIVES

But when you are praying, first forgive anyone you are holding a grudge against, so that your Father in heaven will forgive your sins, too.

Mark 11:25 NLT

Genuine love is an exercise in forgiveness. If we wish to build lasting relationships, we must learn how to forgive. Why? Because our loved ones are imperfect (as are we). How often must we forgive our family and friends? More times than we can count. Why? Because that's what God wants us to do.

Perhaps granting forgiveness is hard for you. If so, you are not alone. Genuine, lasting forgiveness is often difficult to achieve—difficult but not impossible. Thankfully, with God's help, all things are possible, and that includes forgiveness. But, even though God is willing to help, He expects you to do some of the work. And make no mistake: forgiveness is work, which is okay with God. He knows that the payoffs are worth the effort.

We pardon to the degree that we love.

François de la Rochefoucauld

A HELPING HAND

The greatest among you will be your servant. For whoever exalts himself will be humbled, and whoever humbles himself will be exalted.

Matthew 23:11-12 NIV

Jesus has much to teach us about generosity. He teaches that the most esteemed men and women are not the self-congratulatory leaders of society but are, instead, the humblest of servants. If you were being graded on generosity, how would you score? Would you earn "A"s in philanthropy and humility? Hopefully so. But if your grades could stand a little improvement, this is the perfect day to begin.

Today, you may feel the urge to hoard your blessings. Don't do it. Instead, give generously to your neighbors, and do so without fanfare. Find a need and fill it . . . humbly. Lend a helping hand and share a word of kindness . . . anonymously. This is God's way.

We worship God through service. The authentic server views each opportunity to lead or serve as an opportunity to worship God.

Bill Hybels

THE ULTIMATE INSTRUCTION MANUAL

He who scorns instruction will pay for it, but he who respects a command is rewarded.

Proverbs 13:13 NIV

The Holy Bible contains thorough instructions which, if followed, lead to fulfillment, righteousness, and salvation. But, if we choose to ignore God's commandments, the results are as predictable as they are tragic.

A righteous life has many components: faith, honesty, generosity, love, kindness, humility, gratitude, and worship, to name but a few. If we seek to follow the steps of our Savior, Jesus Christ, we must seek to live according to His commandments. Let us follow God's commandments, and let us conduct our lives in such a way that we might be shining examples for those who have not yet found Christ.

Bible history is filled with people who began the race with great success but failed at the end because they disregarded God's rules.

Warren Wiersbe

ADDITIONAL RESPONSIBILITIES

The man who had received the five talents brought the other five. "Master," he said, "you entrusted me with five talents. See, I have gained five more." His master replied, "Well done, good and faithful servant! You have been faithful with a few things; I will put you in charge of many things. Come and share your master's happiness!"

Matthew 25:20-21 NIV

God has promised us this: when we do our duties in small matters, He will give us additional responsibilities. Sometimes, those responsibilities come when God changes the course of our lives so that we may better serve Him. Sometimes, our rewards come in the form of temporary setbacks that lead, in turn, to greater victories. Sometimes, God rewards us by answering "no" to our prayers so that He can say "yes" to a far grander request that we, with our limited understanding, would never have thought to ask for.

If you seek to be God's servant in great matters, be faithful, be patient, and be dutiful in smaller matters. Then step back and watch as God surprises you with the spectacular creativity of His infinite wisdom and His perfect plan.

UP FOR THE CHALLENGE

I will be your God throughout your lifetime—until your hair is white with age. I made you, and I will care for you. I will carry you along and save you.

Isaiah 46:4 NLT

God has promised to lift you up and guide your steps if you let Him do so. God has promised that when you entrust your life to Him completely and without reservation, He will give you the strength to meet any challenge, the courage to face any trial, and the wisdom to live in His righteousness.

God's hand uplifts those who turn their hearts and prayers to Him. Will you count yourself among that number? Will you accept God's peace and wear God's armor against the temptations and distractions of our dangerous world? If you do, you can live courageously and optimistically, knowing that you have been forever touched by the loving, unfailing, uplifting hand of God.

He can accomplish anything He chooses to do. If He ever asks you to do something, He Himself will enable you to do it.

Henry Blackaby

BUILDING SELF-ESTEEM

And let us not grow weary while doing good, for in due season we shall reap if we do not lose heart.

Galatians 6:9 NKJV

Would you like to make the world a better place and feel better about yourself at the same time? If so, you can start by practicing the Golden Rule.

The Bible teaches us to treat other people with respect, kindness, courtesy, and love. When we do, we make other people happy, we make God happy, and we feel better about ourselves.

So if you're wondering how to make the world—and your world—a better place, here's a great place to start: let the Golden Rule be your rule. And if you want to know how to treat other people, ask the person you see every time you glance in the mirror.

When you launch an act of kindness out into the crosswinds of life, it will blow kindness back to you.

Dennis Swanberg

A GOD-MADE MAN

Respecting the Lord and not being proud will bring you wealth, honor, and life.

Proverbs 22:4 NCV

We have heard the phrase on countless occasions: "He's a self-made man." In truth, none of us are self-made. We all owe countless debts that we can never repay. Our first debt, of course, is to our Father in heaven—who has given us everything that we are and will ever be—and to His Son who sacrificed His own life so that we might live eternally. We are also indebted to ancestors, parents, teachers, friends, spouses, family members, co-workers, fellow believers . . . and the list, of course, goes on.

Most of us, it seems, are more than willing to stick out our chests and say, "Look at me; I did that!" But in our better moments, in the quiet moments when we search the depths of our own hearts, we know better. Whatever "it" is, God did that. And He deserves the credit.

Humility is a grace in the soul. It is indescribable wealth, a name and a gift from God.

John Climacus

THE BREAD OF LIFE

Then Jesus said, "I am the bread that gives life. Whoever comes to me will never be hungry, and whoever believes in me will never be thirsty."

John 6:35 NCV

He was the Son of God, but He wore a crown of thorns. He was the Savior of mankind, yet He was put to death on the cross. He offered His healing touch to an unsaved world, and yet the same hands that had healed the sick and raised the dead were pierced with nails.

Jesus Christ, the Son of God, was born into humble circumstances. He walked this earth, not as a ruler of men, but as the Savior of mankind. His crucifixion, a torturous punishment that was intended to end His life and His reign, instead became the pivotal event in the history of all humanity.

Jesus is the bread of life. Accept His grace. Share His love. And follow in His footsteps.

Our Lord is the Bread of Life. His proportions are perfect. There never was too much or too little of anything about Him. Feed on Him for a well-balanced ration. All the vitamins and calories are there.

Vance Havner

THE VOICE OF GOD

Listen in silence before me . . . .

Isaiah 41:1 NLT

Sometimes God speaks loudly and clearly. More often, He speaks in a quiet voice—and if you are wise, you will be listening carefully when He does. To do so, you must carve out quiet moments each day to study His Word and sense His direction.

Can you quiet yourself long enough to listen to your conscience? Are you attuned to the subtle guidance of your intuition? Are you willing to pray sincerely and then to wait quietly for God's response? Hopefully so. Usually God refrains from sending His messages on stone tablets or city billboards. More often, He communicates in subtler ways. If you sincerely desire to hear His voice, you must listen carefully, and you must do so in the silent corners of your quiet, willing heart.

In prayer, the ear is of first importance. It is of equal importance with the tongue, but the ear must be named first. We must listen to God.

S. D. Gordon

MANKIND'S TREASURE HUNT

For where your treasure is, there your heart will be also.

Luke 12:34 NKJV

All of mankind is engaged in a colossal, worldwide treasure hunt. Some people seek treasure from earthly sources, treasures such as wealth or public acclaim; others seek God's treasures by making Him the cornerstone of their lives.

What kind of treasure hunter are you? Are you so caught up in the demands of everyday living that you sometimes allow the search for worldly treasures to become your primary focus? If so, it's time to think long and hard about what you value, and why. All the items on your daily to-do list are not created equal. That's why you must put first things first by placing God in His rightful place: first place. The world's treasures are difficult to find and difficult to keep; God's treasures are ever-present and everlasting. Which treasures, then, will you claim as your own?

Greed is enslaving. The more you have, the more you want—until eventually avarice consumes you.

Kay Arthur

WISDOM IN A DONUT SHOP

My cup runs over. Surely goodness and mercy shall follow me all the days of my life; and I will dwell in the house of the Lord *Forever.*

Psalm 23:5-6 NKJV

Many years ago, this rhyme was posted on the wall of a small donut shop:

As you travel through life brother,
Whatever be your goal,
Keep your eye upon the donut,
And not upon the hole.

These simple words remind us of a profound truth: we should spend more time looking at the things we have, not worrying about the things we don't have.

When you think about it, you've got more blessings than you can count. So make it a habit to thank God for the gifts He's given you, not the gifts you wish He'd given you.

Other men see only a hopeless end, but the Christian rejoices in an endless hope.

Gilbert M. Beeken

PLEASING GOD

But neither exile nor homecoming is the main thing. Cheerfully pleasing God is the main thing, and that's what we aim to do, regardless of our conditions.

2 Corinthians 5:9 MSG

When God made you, He equipped you with an array of talents and abilities that are uniquely yours. It's up to you to discover those talents and to use them, but sometimes the world will encourage you to do otherwise. At times, society will attempt to cubbyhole you, to standardize you, and to make you fit into a particular, preformed mold. Sometimes, because you're an imperfect human being, you may become so wrapped up in meeting society's expectations that you fail to focus on God's expectations. To do so is a mistake of major proportions—don't make it.

Who will you try to please today: God or man? Your primary obligation is not to please imperfect men and women. Your obligation is to strive diligently to meet the expectations of an all-knowing and perfect God. Trust Him always. Love Him always. Praise Him always. And seek to please Him. Always.

COMMUNITY LIFE

Regarding life together and getting along with each other, you don't need me to tell you what to do. You're God-taught in these matters. Just love one another!

1 Thessalonians 4:9 MSG

As we travel along life's road, we build lifelong relationships with a small, dear circle of family and friends. And how best do we build and maintain these relationships? By following the Word of God. Healthy relationships are built upon honesty, compassion, responsible behavior, trust, and optimism. Healthy relationships are built upon the Golden Rule. Healthy relationships are built upon sharing and caring. All of these principles are found time and time again in God's Holy Word. When we read God's Word and follow His commandments, we enrich our own lives and the lives of those who are closest to us.

Horizontal relationships—relationships between people—are crippled at the outset unless the vertical relationship—the relationship between each person and God—is in place.

Ed Young

SO MANY TEMPTATIONS

But remember that the temptations that come into your life are no different from what others experience. And God is faithful. He will keep the temptation from becoming so strong that you can't stand up against it. When you are tempted, he will show you a way out so that you will not give in to it.

1 Corinthians 10:13 NLT

This world is filled to the brim with temptations. Some of these temptations are small; eating a second scoop of ice cream, for example, is tempting, but not very dangerous. Other temptations, however, are not nearly so harmless. The devil is working 24/7, and he's causing pain and heartache in more ways than ever before. Thankfully, in the battle against Satan, we are never alone. God is always with us, and He gives us the power to resist temptation whenever we ask Him for the strength to do so.

In a letter to believers, Peter offered a stern warning: "Your adversary, the devil, prowls around like a roaring lion, seeking someone to devour" (I Peter 5:8 NASB). As Christians, we must take that warning seriously, and we must behave accordingly.

THE ANSWER TO ADVERSITY

I have heard your prayer, I have seen your tears; surely I will heal you.

2 Kings 20:5 NKJV

From time to time, all of us must endure discouragement and defeat. And, we sometimes experience life-changing personal losses that leave us reeling. When we do, God stands ready to protect us. When we are troubled, we must call upon God, and, in His own time and according to His own plan, He will heal us.

Are you anxious? Take those anxieties to God. Are you troubled? Take your troubles to Him. Does your world seem to be trembling beneath your feet? Seek protection from the One who cannot be moved. The same God who created the universe will protect you if you ask Him . . . so ask Him.

If God sends us on stony paths, he provides strong shoes.

Corrie ten Boom

TERMINATING THE TANTRUM

Bad temper is contagious—don't get infected.

Proverbs 22:25 MSG

Temper tantrums are usually unproductive, unattractive, unforgettable, and unnecessary. Perhaps that's why Proverbs 16:32 states that, "Controlling your temper is better than capturing a city" (NCV).

If you've allowed anger to become a regular visitor at your house, today you must pray for wisdom, for patience, and for a heart that is so filled with love and forgiveness that it contains no room for bitterness. God will help you terminate your tantrums if you ask Him to. And God can help you perfect your ability to be patient if you ask Him to. So ask Him, and then wait patiently for the ever-more-patient you to arrive.

The deadly cancer of anger from which so much harm grows: It makes us unlike ourselves, makes us like timber wolves or furies from hell; drives us forth headlong upon the points of swords, makes us blindly run forth after other men's destruction as we hasten toward our own ruin.

St. Thomas More

LIVING IN AN ANXIOUS WORLD

Cast all your anxiety on him because he cares for you.

1 Peter 5:7 NIV

We live in a world that often breeds anxiety and fear. When we come face-to-face with tough times, we may fall prey to discouragement, doubt, or depression. But our Father in heaven has other plans. God has promised that we may lead lives of abundance, not anxiety. In fact, His Word instructs us to "be anxious for nothing" (Philippians 4:6). But how can we put our fears to rest? By taking those fears to God and leaving them there.

As you face the challenges of daily life, you may find yourself becoming anxious, troubled, discouraged, or fearful. If so, turn every one of your concerns over to your Heavenly Father. The same God who created the universe will comfort you if you ask Him . . . so ask Him and trust Him. And then watch in amazement as your anxieties melt into the warmth of His loving hands.

One of the main missions of God is to free us from the debilitating bonds of fear and anxiety. God's heart is broken when He sees us so demoralized and weighed down by fear.

Bill Hybels

NEW BEGINNINGS

Do not remember the former things, nor consider the things of old. Behold, I will do a new thing.

Isaiah 43:18-19 NKJV

Each new day offers countless opportunities to serve God, to seek His will, and to obey His teachings. But each day also offers countless opportunities to stray from God's commandments and to wander far from His path.

Sometimes, we wander aimlessly in a wilderness of our own making, but God has better plans for us. And, whenever we ask Him to renew our strength and guide our steps, He does so.

Consider this day a new beginning. Consider it a fresh start, a renewed opportunity to serve your Creator with willing hands and a loving heart. Ask God to renew your sense of purpose as He guides your steps. Today is a glorious opportunity to serve your Father in heaven. Seize that opportunity while you can; tomorrow may indeed be too late.

No matter how badly we have failed, we can always get up and begin again. Our God is the God of new beginnings.

Warren Wiersbe

SMILES AND MORE SMILES

Jacob said, "For what a relief it is to see your friendly smile. It is like seeing the smile of God!"

Genesis 33:10 NLT

Life should never be taken for granted. Each day is a priceless gift from God and should be treated as such.

Hannah Whitall Smith observed, "How changed our lives would be if we could only fly through the days on wings of surrender and trust!" And Clement of Alexandria noted, "All our life is a celebration for us; we are convinced, in fact, that God is always everywhere. We sing while we work . . . we pray while we carry out all life's other occupations." These words remind us that this day is God's creation, a gift to be treasured and savored.

Today, let us celebrate life with smiles on our faces and kind words on our lips. After all, this is God's day, and He has given us clear instructions for its use. We are commanded to rejoice and be glad. So, with no further ado, let the celebration begin . . . .

OUR CHILDREN, OUR HOPE

Let the little children come to Me; don't stop them, for the kingdom of God belongs to such as these.

Mark 10:14 HCSB

Every child is different, but every child is similar in this respect: he or she is a priceless gift from the Father above. And, with the Father's gift comes immense responsibilities.

Our children are our nation's most precious resource. And, as responsible parents, we must create homes in which the future generation can grow and flourish.

Today, let us pray for our children . . . all of them. Let us pray for children here at home and for children around the world. Every child is God's child. May we, as concerned adults, behave—and pray—accordingly.

Let us look upon our children; let us love them and train them as children of the covenant and children of the promise. These are the children of God.

Andrew Murray

LIVING IN CHRIST'S LOVE

And now, children, stay with Christ. Live deeply in Christ. Then we'll be ready for him when he appears, ready to receive him with open arms, with no cause for red-faced guilt or lame excuses when he arrives. Once you're convinced that he is right and righteous, you'll recognize that all who practice righteousness are God's true children.

1 John 2:28-29 MSG

God's love for us is unconditional. No matter what we have done good or bad God's love is steady and sure. Even though we are imperfect, fallible human beings, even though we have fallen far short of God's commandments, Christ loves us still. His love is perfect; it does not waver—it does not change. Our task, as believers, is to accept Christ's love and to encourage others to do likewise.

In today's troubled world, we all need the love and the peace that is found through the Son of God. Thankfully, Christ's love has no limits. We, in turn, should love Him with no limits, beginning now and ending never.

FEEDING THE CHURCH

The church, you see, is not peripheral to the world; the world is peripheral to the church. The church is Christ's body, in which he speaks and acts, by which he fills everything with his presence.

Ephesians 1:23 MSG

One way that we come to know God is by involving ourselves in His church.

In the Book of Acts, Luke reminds us to "feed the church of God" (20:28). As Christians who have been saved by a loving, compassionate Creator, we are compelled not only to worship Him in our hearts but also to worship Him in the presence of fellow believers.

Do you feed the church of God? Do you attend regularly, and are you an active participant? The answer to these questions will have a profound impact on the quality and direction of your spiritual journey.

So do yourself a favor: become actively involved in your church. Don't just go to church out of habit. Go to church out of a sincere desire to know and worship God. When you do, you'll be blessed by the One who sent His Son to die so that you might have everlasting life.

THE POWER OF PRAYER

The intense prayer of the righteous is very powerful.

James 5:16 HCSB

"The power of prayer": these words are so familiar, yet sometimes we forget what they mean. Prayer is a powerful tool for communicating with our Creator; it is an opportunity to commune with the Giver of all things good. Prayer helps us find strength for today and hope for the future. Prayer is not a thing to be taken lightly or to be used infrequently.

The quality of your spiritual life will be in direct proportion to the quality of your prayer life. Prayer changes things, and it changes you. Today, instead of turning things over in your mind, turn them over to God in prayer. Instead of worrying about your next decision, ask God to lead the way. Pray constantly about things great and small. God is listening, and He wants to hear from you now.

Where there is much prayer, there will be much of the Spirit; where there is much of the Spirit, there will be ever-increasing power.

Andrew Murray

THE MORNING WATCH

Every morning he wakes me. He teaches me to listen like a student. The Lord God helps me learn . . . .

Isaiah 50:4-5 NCV

Each new day is a gift from God, and if you are wise, you will spend a few quiet moments each morning thanking the Giver.

Warren Wiersbe writes, "Surrender your mind to the Lord at the beginning of each day." And that's sound advice. When you begin each day with your head bowed and your heart lifted, you are reminded of God's love, His protection, and His commandments. Then, you can align your priorities for the coming day with the teachings and commandments that God has placed upon your heart.

So, if you've acquired the unfortunate habit of trying to "squeeze" God into the corners of your life, it's time to reshuffle the items on your to-do list by placing God first. And if you haven't already done so, form the habit of spending quality time with your Father in heaven. He deserves it . . . and so do you.

MOVING ON

You have heard it said, "Love your neighbor and hate your enemy." But I tell you: Love your enemies and pray for those who persecute you, that you may be sons of your Father in heaven.

Matthew 5:43-45 NIV

Sometimes, people can be discourteous and cruel. Sometimes people can be unfair, unkind, and unappreciative. Sometimes people get angry and frustrated. So what's a Christian to do? God's answer is straightforward: forgive, forget, and move on. In Luke 6:37, Jesus instructs, "Do not judge, and you will not be judged. Do not condemn, and you will not be condemned. Forgive, and you will be forgiven" (HCSB).

Today and every day, make sure that you're quick to forgive others for their shortcomings. And when other people misbehave (as they most certainly will from time to time), don't pay too much attention. Just forgive those people as quickly as you can, and try to move on . . . as quickly as you can.

When life is difficult, God wants us to have a faith that trusts and waits.

Kay Arthur

THE NEED FOR SELF-DISCIPLINE

Do you not know that those who run in a race all run, but only one receives the prize? Run in such a way that you may win. Everyone who competes in the games exercises self-control in all things.

1 Corinthians 9:24-25 NASB

God is clear: we must exercise self-discipline in all matters. Self-discipline is not simply a proven way to get ahead, it's also an integral part of God's plan for our lives. If we genuinely seek to be faithful stewards of our time, our talents, and our resources, we must adopt a disciplined approach to life. Otherwise, our talents are wasted and our resources are squandered.

Our greatest rewards result from hard work and perseverance. May we, as disciplined believers, be willing to work for the rewards we so earnestly desire.

As we seek to become disciples of Jesus Christ, we should never forget that the word disciple is directly related to the word discipline. To be a disciple of the Lord Jesus Christ is to know his discipline.

Dennis Swanberg

BEYOND ENVY

Therefore, laying aside all malice, all deceit, hypocrisy, envy, and all evil speaking, as newborn babes, desire the pure milk of the word, that you may grow thereby.

1 Peter 2:1-2 NKJV

In a competitive, cut-throat world, it is easy to become envious of other's success. But it's wrong.

We know intuitively that envy is wrong, but because we are frail, imperfect human beings, we may find ourselves struggling with feelings of envy or resentment, or both. These feelings may be especially forceful when we see other people experience unusually good fortune.

Have you recently felt the pangs of envy creeping into your heart? If so, it's time to focus on the marvelous things that God has done for you and your family. And just as importantly, you must refrain from preoccupying yourself with the blessings that God has chosen to give others.

So here's a surefire formula for a happier, healthier life: Count your own blessings and let your neighbors counts theirs. It's the godly way to live.

WE ARE ALL ROLE MODELS

You are the light that gives light to the world. In the same way, you should be a light for other people. Live so that they will see the good things you do and will praise your Father in heaven.

Matthew 5:14, 16 NCV

All of us are examples—examples that should be emulated . . . or not. Hopefully, the lives we lead and the choices we make will serve as enduring examples of the spiritual abundance that is available to all who worship God and obey His commandments.

Ask yourself this question: Are you the kind of role model that you would want to emulate? If so, congratulations. But if certain aspects of your behavior could stand improvement, the best day to begin your self-improvement regimen is this one. Because whether you realize it or not, people you love are watching your behavior, and they're learning how to live. You owe it to them—and to yourself—to live righteously and well.

I'd rather see a sermon than hear one any day; I'd rather one should walk with me than merely tell the way.

Edgar A. Guest

FAITH VERSUS FEAR

Don't be afraid, because I am your God. I will make you strong and will help you; I will support you with my right hand that saves you.

Isaiah 41:10 NCV

A terrible storm rose quickly on the Sea of Galilee, and the disciples were afraid. Although they had witnessed many miracles, the disciples feared for their lives, so they turned to Jesus, and He calmed the waters and the wind.

The next time you find yourself facing a fear-provoking situation, remember that the One who calmed the wind and the waves is also your personal Savior. Then ask yourself which is stronger: your faith or your fear. The answer should be obvious. So, when the storm clouds form overhead and you find yourself being tossed on the stormy seas of life, remember this: Wherever you are, God is there, too. And, because He cares for you, you are protected.

Courage faces fear and thereby masters it. Cowardice represses fear and is thereby mastered by it.

Martin Luther King

THE CORNERSTONE

Let us fix our eyes on Jesus, the author and perfecter of our faith, who for the joy set before him endured the cross, scorning its shame, and sat down at the right hand of the throne of God.

Hebrews 12:2 NIV

This day—and every day hereafter—is a chance to celebrate the life that God has given you. It's also a chance to give thanks to the One who has offered you more blessings than you can possibly count. What is your focus today? Are you willing to focus your thoughts and energies on God's blessings and upon His will for your life? Or will you turn your thoughts to other things?

Today, why not focus your thoughts on the joy that is rightfully yours in Christ? Why not take time to celebrate God's glorious creation? Why not trust your hopes instead of your fears? When you do, you will think optimistically about yourself and your world . . . and you can then share your optimism with others. They'll be better for it, and so will you. But not necessarily in that order.

Give me the person who says, "This one thing I do, and not these fifty things I dabble in."

D. L. Moody

THE CHOICE TO FORGIVE

You have heard that it was said, "Love your neighbor and hate your enemy." But I tell you: Love your enemies and pray for those who persecute you.

Matthew 5:43-44 NIV

Forgiveness is a choice. We can either choose to forgive those who have injured us, or not. When we obey God by offering forgiveness to His children, we are blessed. But when we allow bitterness and resentment to poison our hearts, we are tortured by our own shortsightedness.

Do you harbor resentment against anyone? If so, you are faced with an important decision: whether or not to forgive the person who has hurt you. God's instructions are clear: He commands you to forgive. And the time to forgive is now because tomorrow may be too late . . . for you.

All the heart of God is the desire to give and to forgive.

Richard Foster

Mercy imitates God and disappoints Satan.

St. John Chrysostom

CARING FOR THE DOWNTRODDEN

I tell you the truth, whatever you did for one of the least of these brothers of mine, you did for me.

Matthew 25:40 NIV

How fortunate we are to live in a land of opportunities and possibilities. But, for many people around the world, opportunities are scarce at best. In too many corners of the globe, hardworking men and women struggle mightily to provide food and shelter for their families.

When we care for the downtrodden, we follow in the footsteps of Christ. And, when we show compassion for those who suffer, we abide by the commandments of the One who created us. May we, who have been given so much, hear the Word of God . . . and may we follow it.

If you want to be truly happy, you won't find it on an endless quest for more stuff. You'll find it in receiving God's generosity and the passing that generosity along.

Bill Hybels

HIS AWESOME CREATION

And to every beast of the earth and to every bird of the sky and to every thing that moves on the earth which has life . . . God saw all that He had made, and behold, it was very good.

Genesis 1:30-31 NASB

When we consider God's glorious universe, we marvel at the miracle of nature. The smallest seedlings and grandest stars are all part of God's infinite creation. God has placed His handiwork on display for all to see, and if we are wise, we will make time each day to celebrate the world that surrounds us.

Today, as you fulfill the demands of everyday life, pause to consider the majesty of heaven and earth. It is as miraculous as it is beautiful, as incomprehensible as it is breathtaking.

The Psalmist reminds us that the heavens are a declaration of God's glory (Psalm 19:1). May we never cease to praise the Father for a universe that stands as an awesome testimony to His presence and His power.

God expresses His love through creation.

Charles Stanley

LIMITLESS POWER, LIMITLESS LOVE

I pray also that you will have greater understanding in your heart so you will know the hope to which he has called us and that you will know how rich and glorious are the blessings God has promised his holy people. And you will know that God's power is very great for us who believe. That power is the same as the great strength.

Ephesians 1:18-19 NCV

Because God's power is limitless, it is far beyond the comprehension of mortal minds. Yet even though we cannot fully understand the awesome power of God, we can praise it. When we worship God with faith and assurance, when we place Him at the absolute center of our lives, we invite His love into our hearts. In turn, we grow to love Him more deeply as we sense His love for us. St. Augustine wrote, "I love you, Lord, not doubtingly, but with absolute certainty. Your Word beat upon my heart until I fell in love with you, and now the universe and everything in it tells me to love you."

Let us pray that we, too, will turn our hearts to the Creator, knowing with certainty that His heart has ample room for each of us, and that we, in turn, must make room in our hearts for Him.

WAITING FOR GOD

The Lord *is good to those who wait for Him, To the soul who seeks Him. It is good that one should hope and wait quietly For the salvation of the* Lord.

Lamentations 3:25-26 NKJV

We human beings are so impatient. We know what we want, and we know exactly when we want it: RIGHT NOW! But, God knows better. He has created a world that unfolds according to His own timetable, not ours.

As Christians, we must be patient as we wait for God to show us the wonderful plans that He has in store for us. And while we're waiting for God to make His plans clear, let's keep praying and keep giving thanks to the One who has given us more blessings than we can count.

Grass that is here today and gone tomorrow does not require much time to mature. A big oak tree that lasts for generations requires much more time to grow and mature. God is concerned about your life through eternity. Allow Him to take all the time He needs.

Henry Blackaby

IN GOD WE TRUST

And my God shall supply all your need according to His riches in glory by Christ Jesus.

Philippians 4:19 NKJV

All of us experience adversity, disappointments, and hardship. Sometimes we bring these hardships upon ourselves, and sometimes we are victimized by circumstances that we cannot control and cannot fully understand. As human beings with limited insight, we can never completely comprehend the will of our Father in heaven. But as believers in a benevolent God, we must always trust His providence. When Jesus went to the Mount of Olives, as described in Luke 22, He poured out His heart to God. Jesus knew of the agony that He was destined to endure, but He also knew that God's will must be done. We, like our Savior, face trials that bring fear and trembling to the very depths of our souls, but like Christ we, too, must seek God's will, not our own.

Have you been touched by a personal tragedy that you cannot understand? If so, it's time to accept the unchangeable past . . . and it's time to trust God completely. When you do, you'll reclaim the peace—His peace—that can and should be yours.

A WALK WITH GOD

I've laid down a pattern for you. What I've done, you do.

John 13:15 MSG

Each day, we are confronted with countless opportunities to serve God and to follow in the footsteps of His Son. When we do, our Heavenly Father guides our steps and blesses our endeavors. As citizens of a fast-changing world, we face challenges that sometimes leave us feeling overworked, overcommitted, and overwhelmed. But God has different plans for us. He intends that we slow down long enough to praise Him and to glorify His Son. When we do, He lifts our spirits and enriches our lives.

Today provides a glorious opportunity to place yourself in the service of the One who is the Giver of all blessings. May you seek His will, may you trust His Word, and may you walk in the footsteps of His Son.

Christ is to be sought and bought with any pains, at any price; we can not buy this gold too dear. He is a jewel worth more than a thousand worlds. Get him, and get all; miss him and miss all.

Thomas Brooks

FORGIVING AND FORGETTING

Real wisdom, God's wisdom, begins with a holy life and is characterized by getting along with others. It is gentle and reasonable, overflowing with mercy and blessings.

James 3:17 MSG

Do you have a tough time forgiving and forgetting? If so, welcome to the club. Most of us find it difficult to forgive the people who have hurt us. And that's too bad because life would be much simpler if we could forgive people "once and for all" and be done with it. Yet forgiveness is seldom that easy. Usually, the decision to forgive is straightforward, but the process of forgiving is more difficult. Forgiveness is a journey that requires time, perseverance, and prayer.

If you sincerely wish to forgive someone, pray for that person. And then pray for yourself by asking God to heal your heart. Don't expect forgiveness to be easy or quick, but rest assured: with God as your partner, you can forgive . . . and you will.

Forgiving is a gift God has given us for healing ourselves before we are ready to help anyone else.

Dr. Lewis Smedes

IN HIS HANDS

Don't brashly announce what you're going to do tomorrow; you don't know the first thing about tomorrow.

Proverbs 27:1 MSG

The old saying is both familiar and true: "Man proposes and God disposes." Our world unfolds according to God's plans, not our wishes. Thus, boasting about future events is to be avoided by those who acknowledge God's sovereignty over all things.

Are you planning for a better tomorrow for yourself and your family? If so, you are to be congratulated: God rewards forethought in the same way that He often punishes impulsiveness. But as you make your plans, do so with humility, with gratitude, and with trust in your Heavenly Father. His hand directs the future; to think otherwise is both arrogant and naïve.

That we may not complain of what is, let us see God's hand in all events; and, that we may not be afraid of what shall be, let us see all events in God's hand.

Matthew Henry

HIS INTIMATE LOVE

As the Father loved Me, I also have loved you; abide in My love.

John 15:9 NKJV

St. Augustine observed, "God loves each of us as if there were only one of us." Do you believe those words? Do you seek an intimate, one-on-one relationship with your Heavenly Father, or are you satisfied to keep Him at a "safe" distance?

Sometimes, in the crush of our daily duties, God may seem far away, but He is not. God is everywhere we have ever been and everywhere we will ever go. He is with us night and day; He knows our thoughts and our prayers. And, when we earnestly seek Him, we will find Him because He is here, waiting patiently for us to reach out to Him. May we reach out to Him today and always. And may we praise Him for the glorious gifts that have transformed us today and forever.

God wants to emancipate his people; he wants to set them free. He wants his people to be not slaves but sons. He wants them governed not by law but by love.

Max Lucado

YOUR WAY OR GOD'S WAY

A man's heart plans his way, but the LORD *directs his steps.*

Proverbs 16:9 NKJV

The popular song "My Way" is a perfectly good tune, but it's not a perfect guide for life here on earth. If you're looking for life's perfect prescription, you'd better forget about doing things your way and start doing things God's way. The most important decision of your life is, of course, your commitment to accept Jesus Christ as your personal Lord and Savior. And once your eternal destiny is secured, you will undoubtedly ask yourself the question, "What now, Lord?" If you earnestly seek God's will for your life, you will find it . . . in time.

Sometimes, God's plans are crystal clear; sometimes they are not. So be patient, keep searching, and keep praying. If you do, then in time, God will answer your prayers and make His plans known. You'll discover those plans by doing things His way . . . and you'll be eternally grateful that you did.

YOUR PERSONAL JOURNEY

Know the love of Christ which surpasses knowledge, that you may be filled up to all the fullness of God.

Ephesians 3:19 NASB

The journey toward spiritual maturity lasts a lifetime. As Christians, we can and should continue to grow in the love and the knowledge of our Savior as long as we live. When we cease to grow, either emotionally or spiritually, we do ourselves a profound disservice. But, if we study God's Word, if we obey His commandments, and if we live in the center of His will, we will not be "stagnant" believers; we will, instead, be healthy, growing Christians.

Life is a series of decisions. Each day, we make countless decisions that can bring us closer to God . . . or not. When we live according to the principles contained in God's Holy Word, we embark upon a journey of spiritual maturity that results in life abundant and life eternal.

Being a Christian means accepting the terms of creation, accepting God as our maker and redeemer, and growing day by day into an increasingly glorious creature in Christ.

Eugene Peterson

MAKING PEACE WITH YOUR PAST

The Lord says, "Forget what happened before, and do not think about the past. Look at the new thing I am going to do. It is already happening. Don't you see it? I will make a road in the desert and rivers in the dry land."

Isaiah 43:18-19 NCV

Have you made peace with your past? If so, congratulations. But, if you are mired in the quicksand of regret, it's time to plan your escape. How can you do so? By accepting what has been and by trusting God for what will be

Because you are human, you may be slow to forget yesterday's disappointments. But, if you sincerely seek to focus your hopes and energies on the future, then you must find ways to accept the past, no matter how difficult it may be to do so. So, if you have not yet made peace with the past, today is the day to declare an end to all hostilities. When you do, you can then turn your thoughts to wondrous promises of God and to the glorious future that He has in store for you.

You cannot change the past, but you can control your own attitude.

Barbara Johnson

PRAISE HIM

Praise the L*ORD. Give thanks to the* L*ORD, for he is good; his love endures forever.*

Psalm 106:1 NIV

Sometimes, in our rush "to get things done," we simply don't stop long enough to pause and thank our Creator for the countless blessings He has bestowed upon us. But when we slow down and express our gratitude to the One who made us, we enrich our own lives and the lives of those around us.

Thanksgiving should become a habit, a regular part of our daily routines. God has blessed us beyond measure, and we owe Him everything, including our eternal praise. Let us praise Him today, tomorrow, and throughout eternity.

Maintaining a focus on God will take our praise to heights that nothing else can.

Jeff Walling

Today you will encounter God's creation. When you see the beauty around you, let each detail remind you to lift your head in praise.

Max Lucado

SOLVING PROBLEMS

People who do what is right may have many problems, but the Lord will solve them all.

Psalm 34:19 NCV

Life is an exercise in problem-solving. The question is not whether we will encounter problems; the real question is how we will choose to address them. When it comes to solving the problems of everyday living, we often know precisely what needs to be done, but we may be slow in doing it—especially if what needs to be done is difficult or uncomfortable for us. So we put off till tomorrow what should be done today.

The words of Psalm 34 remind us that the Lord solves problems for "people who do what is right." And usually, doing "what is right" means doing the uncomfortable work of confronting our problems sooner rather than later. So with no further ado, let the problem-solving begin . . . now.

We are all faced with a series of great opportunities, brilliantly disguised as unsolvable problems. Unsolvable without God's wisdom, that is.

Charles Swindoll

GOD'S TIMING

Humble yourselves, therefore, under God's mighty hand, that he may lift you up in due time.

1 Peter 5:6 NIV

Sometimes, the hardest thing to do is to wait. This is especially true when we're in a hurry and when we want things to happen now, if not sooner! But God's plan does not always happen in the way that we would like or at the time of our own choosing. Our task—as believing Christians who trust in a benevolent, all knowing Father—is to wait patiently for God to reveal Himself.

We human beings are, by nature, impatient. We know what we want, and we know exactly when we want it: RIGHT NOW! But, God knows better. He has created a world that unfolds according to His own timetable, not ours . . . thank goodness!

Events of all sorts creep or fly exactly as God pleases.

William Cowper

Will not the Lord's time be better than your time?

C. H. *Spurgeon*

A ONE-OF-A-KIND TREASURE

Every word of God is flawless; he is a shield to those who take refuge in him.

Proverbs 30:5 NIV

God's Word is a roadmap for life here on earth and for life eternal. As Christians, we are called upon to study God's Holy Word, to trust its promises, to follow its commandments, and to share its Good News with the world.

As believers, we must study the Bible and meditate upon its meaning for our lives. Otherwise, we deprive ourselves of a priceless gift from our Creator. God's Holy Word is, indeed, a transforming, life-changing, one-of-a-kind treasure. And, a passing acquaintance with the Good Book is insufficient for Christians who seek to obey God's Word and to understand His will. After all, neither man nor woman should live by bread alone . . .

The Gospel is not so much a demand as it is an offer, an offer of new life to man by the grace of God.

E. Stanley Jones

THE WORLD'S BEST FRIEND

Greater love has no one than this, that he lay down his life for his friends.

John 15:13 NIV

Our circumstances change, but Jesus does not. Even when the world seems to be trembling between our feet, Jesus remains the spiritual bedrock that cannot be moved.

The old familiar hymn begins, "What a friend we have in Jesus . . . ." No truer words were ever penned. Jesus is the sovereign friend and ultimate Savior of mankind. Christ showed enduring love for His believers by willingly sacrificing His own life so that we might have eternal life. Let us love Him, praise Him, and share His message of salvation with our neighbors and with the world.

The dearest friend on earth is but a mere shadow compared with Jesus Christ.

Oswald Chambers

Jesus came into the world so we could know, once and for all, that God is concerned about the way we live, the way we believe, and the way we die.

Billy Graham

HIS JOY . . . AND OURS

Always be full of joy in the Lord. I say it again—rejoice!

Philippians 4:4 NLT

The Bible makes it clear: God intends that His joy should become our joy. As believers who have been saved by a loving and merciful God, we have every reason to celebrate. Yet sometimes, amid the inevitable hustle and bustle of life here on earth, we can forfeit—albeit temporarily—the joy that God has in store for us.

This day is a gift from the Creator. Let us celebrate it cheerfully; let us worship Him with thanks in our hearts and praise on our lips. Let us raise our thoughts and our prayers to Him. And let us accept the joy that is the spiritual birthright of those who have been touched and saved by the Master's hand.

When I think of God, my heart is so full of joy that the notes leap and dance as they leave my pen; and since God has given me a cheerful heart, I serve him with a cheerful spirit.

Franz Joseph Haydn

A GODLY LEADER

But a good leader plans to do good, and those good things make him a good leader.

Isaiah 32:8 NCV

Our world needs Christian leaders who willingly honor God with their words and their deeds, but not necessarily in that order.

If you seek to be a godly leader, then you must begin by being a worthy example to your family, to your friends, to your church, and to your community. After all, your words of instruction will never ring true unless you yourself are willing to follow them.

Are you the kind of leader whom you would want to follow? If so, congratulations. But if the answer to that question is no, then it's time to improve your leadership skills, beginning with the words that you speak and the example that you set, but not necessarily in that order.

The goal of leadership is to empower the whole people of God to discern and to discharge the Lord's will.

Stanley Grenz

THE WISDOM OF MODERATION

Moderation is better than muscle, self-control better than political power.

Proverbs 16:32 MSG

Moderation and wisdom are traveling companions. If we are wise, we must learn to temper our appetites, our desires, and our impulses. When we do, we are blessed, in part, because God has created a world in which temperance is rewarded and intemperance is inevitably punished.

Would you like to improve your life? Then harness your appetites and restrain your impulses. Moderation is difficult, of course; it is especially difficult in a prosperous society such as ours. But the rewards of moderation are numerous and long-lasting. Claim those rewards today. No one can force you to moderate your appetites. The decision to live temperately (and wisely) is yours and yours alone. And so are the consequences.

We are all created differently. We share a common need to balance the different parts of our lives.

Dr. Walt Larimore

BEING PATIENT WITH OURSELVES

Knowing God leads to self-control. Self-control leads to patient endurance, and patient endurance leads to godliness.

2 Peter 1:6 NLT

Being patient with other people can be difficult. But sometimes, we find it even more difficult to be patient with ourselves. We have high expectations and lofty goals. We want to accomplish things now, not later. And, of course, we want our lives to unfold according to our own timetables, not God's.

Throughout the Bible, we are instructed that patience is the companion of wisdom. God's message, then, is clear: we must be patient with all people, beginning with that particular person who stares back at us each time we gaze into the mirror.

Be patient. God is using today's difficulties to strengthen you for tomorrow. He is equipping you. The God who makes things grow will help you bear fruit.

Max Lucado

YOUR REAL RICHES

He said, "I came naked from my mother's womb, and I will be stripped of everything when I die. The L*ORD gave me everything I had, and the* L*ORD has taken it away. Praise the name of the* L*ORD!"*

Job 1:21 NLT

Martin Luther observed, "Many things I have tried to grasp and have lost. That which I have placed in God's hands I still have." How true. Earthly riches are transitory; spiritual riches are not.

In our demanding world, financial security can be a good thing, but spiritual prosperity is profoundly more important. Certainly we all need the basic necessities of life, but once we've acquired those necessities, enough is enough. Why? Because our real riches are not of this world. We are never really rich until we are rich in spirit.

God's kindness is not like the sunset—brilliant in its intensity, but dying every second. God's generosity keeps coming and coming and coming.

Bill Hybels

REAL REPENTANCE

I preached that they should repent and turn to God and prove their repentance by their deeds.

Acts 26:20 NIV

Who among us has sinned? All of us. But the good news is this: When we do ask God's forgiveness and turn our hearts to Him, He forgives us absolutely and completely.

Genuine repentance requires more than simply offering God apologies for our misdeeds. Real repentance may start with feelings of sorrow and remorse, but it ends only when we turn away from the sin that has heretofore distanced us from our Creator. In truth, we offer our most meaningful apologies to God, not with our words, but with our actions. As long as we are still engaged in sin, we may be "repenting," but we have not fully "repented." So, if there is an aspect of your life that is distancing you from your God, ask for His forgiveness, and—just as importantly—stop sinning. Now.

Repentance involves a radical change of heart and mind in which we agree with God's evaluation of our sin and then take specific action to align ourselves with His will.

Henry Blackaby

OVERCOMING EVERYDAY FRUSTRATIONS

A hot-tempered man stirs up dissention, but a patient man calms a quarrel.

Proverbs 15:18 NIV

Life is full of frustrations: some great and some small. On occasion, you, like Jesus, will confront evil, and when you do, you may respond as He did: vigorously and without reservation. But, more often your frustrations will be of the more mundane variety. As long as you live here on earth, you will face countless opportunities to lose your temper over small, relatively insignificant events: a traffic jam, a spilled cup of coffee, an inconsiderate comment, a broken promise. When you are tempted to lose your temper over the minor inconveniences of life, don't. Turn away from anger, hatred, bitterness, and regret. Turn instead to God. When you do, you'll be following His commandments and giving yourself a priceless gift . . . the gift of peace.

Why lose your temper if, by doing so, you offend God, annoy other people, give yourself a bad time . . . and, in the end, have to find it again?

Josemaria Escriva

WHAT'S MORE POWERFUL: YOUR WALK OR YOUR TALK?

If the way you live isn't consistent with what you believe, then it's wrong.

Romans 14:23 MSG

As Christians, we must do our best to ensure that our actions are accurate reflections of our beliefs. Our theology must be demonstrated, not only by our words but, more importantly, by our actions. In short, we should be practical believers, quick to act whenever we see an opportunity to serve God.

Are you the kind of practical Christian man who is willing to dig in and do what needs to be done when it needs to be done? If so, congratulations: God acknowledges your service and blesses it. But if you find yourself more interested in the fine points of theology than in the needs of your neighbors, it's time to rearrange your priorities. God needs believers who are willing to roll up their sleeves and go to work for Him. Count yourself among that number. Theology is a good thing unless it interferes with God's work. And it's up to you to make certain that your theology doesn't.

A PRESCRIPTION FOR PANIC

Anxiety in the heart of man causes depression, but a good word makes it glad.

Proverbs 12:25 NKJV

We live in a world that sometimes seems to shift beneath our feet. We live in an uncertain world, a world where tragedies can befall even the most godly among us. And we are members of an anxious society, a society in which the changes we face threaten to outpace our abilities to make adjustments. No wonder we sometimes find ourselves beset by feelings of anxiety and panic.

At times, our anxieties may stem from physical causes—chemical imbalances in the brain that result in severe emotional distress or relentless panic attacks. In such cases, medicine offers hope to those who suffer. But oftentimes, our anxieties result from spiritual deficits, not physical ones. And when we're spiritually depleted, the best prescription is found not in the medicine cabinet but deep inside the human heart. What we need is a higher daily dose of God's love, God's peace, and God's presence. And how do we acquire these blessings from our Creator? Through prayer, through meditation, through worship, and through trust.

THE RIGHT KIND OF BEHAVIOR

By this we know that we have come to know Him, if we keep His commandments.

1 John 2:3 NASB

When we seek righteousness in our own lives—and when we seek the companionship of those who do likewise—we reap the spiritual rewards that God intends for us to enjoy. When we behave ourselves as godly men, we honor God. When we live righteously and according to God's commandments, He blesses us in ways that we cannot fully understand.

Today, as you fulfill your responsibilities, hold fast that which is good, and associate yourself with believers who behave themselves in like fashion. When you do, your good works will serve as a powerful example for others and as a worthy offering to your Creator.

Christianity says we were created by a righteous God to flourish and be exhilarated in a righteous environment. God has "wired" us in such a way that the more righteous we are, the more we'll actually enjoy life.

Bill Hybels

YOU ARE BLESSED

I will bless them and the places surrounding my hill. I will send down showers in season; there will be showers of blessings.

Ezekiel 34:26 NIV

If you sat down and began counting your blessings, how long would it take? A very, very long time! Your blessings include life, freedom, family, friends, talents, and possessions, for starters. But, your greatest blessing—a gift that is yours for the asking—is God's gift of salvation through Christ Jesus.

Today, begin making a list of your blessings. You most certainly will not be able to make a complete list, but take a few moments and jot down as many blessings as you can. Then give thanks to the Giver of all good things: God. His love for you is eternal, as are His gifts. And it's never too soon—or too late—to offer Him thanks.

God wants his people to earnestly seek his will and to pray for it, and thus to become agents of the blessing God brings.

James Montgomery Boice

COUNTING YOUR BLESSINGS

Finally brothers, whatever is true, whatever is honorable, whatever is just . . . if there is any moral excellence and if there is any praise—dwell on these things.

Philippians 4:8 HCSB

How will you direct your thoughts today? Will you obey the words of Philippians 4:8 by dwelling upon those things that are honorable, just, and commendable? Or will you allow your thoughts to be hijacked by the negativity that seems to dominate our troubled world? Are you fearful, angry, bored, or worried? Are you so preoccupied with the concerns of this day that you fail to thank God for the promise of eternity? Are you confused, bitter, or pessimistic? If so, God wants to have a little talk with you.

God intends that you experience joy and abundance. So, today and every day hereafter, celebrate the life that God has given you by focusing your thoughts upon those things that are worthy of praise. Today, count your blessings instead of your hardships. And thank the Giver of all things good for gifts that are simply too numerous to count.

ASKING FOR DIRECTIONS

If you need wisdom—if you want to know what God wants you to do—ask him, and he will gladly tell you. He will not resent your asking.

James 1:5 NLT

Jesus made it clear to His disciples: they should petition God to meet their needs. So should we. Genuine, heartfelt prayer produces powerful changes in us and in our world. When we lift our hearts to God, we open ourselves to a never-ending source of divine wisdom and infinite love.

Do you have questions about your future that you simply can't answer? Do you have needs that you simply can't meet by yourself? Do you sincerely seek to know God's unfolding plans for your life? If so, ask Him for direction, for protection, and for strength—and then keep asking Him every day that you live. Whatever your need, no matter how great or small, pray about it and never lose hope. God is not just near; He is here, and He's perfectly capable of answering your prayers. Now, it's up to you to ask.

LOOK UP AND MOVE ON

And be kind and compassionate to one another, forgiving one another, just as God also forgave you in Christ.

Ephesians 4:32 HCSB

Are you mired in the quicksand of bitterness or regret? If so, you are not only disobeying God's Word, you are also wasting your time. The world holds few if any rewards for those who remain angrily focused upon the past. Still, the act of forgiveness is difficult for all but the most saintly men and women.

Being frail, fallible, imperfect human beings, most of us are quick to anger, quick to blame, slow to forgive, and even slower to forget. Yet as Christians, we are commanded to forgive others, just as we, too, have been forgiven.

If there exists even one person—alive or dead—against whom you hold bitter feelings, it's time to forgive. Or, if you are embittered against yourself for some past mistake or shortcoming, it's finally time to forgive yourself and move on. Hatred, bitterness, and regret are not part of God's plan for your life. Forgiveness is.

Bitterness is the trap that snares the hunter.

Max Lucado

THIS IS HIS DAY

This is the day the LORD has made. We will rejoice and be glad in it.

Psalm 118:24 NLT

The 118th Psalm reminds us that today, like every other day, is a cause for celebration. God gives us this day; He fills it to the brim with possibilities, and He challenges us to use it for His purposes. The day is presented to us fresh and clean at midnight, free of charge, but we must beware: Today is a non-renewable resource—once it's gone, it's gone forever. Our responsibility, of course, is to use this day in the service of God's will and according to His commandments.

Today, treasure the time that God has given you. Give Him the glory and the praise and the thanksgiving that He deserves. And search for the hidden possibilities that God has placed along your path. This day is a priceless gift from God, so use it joyfully and encourage others to do likewise.

All our life is a celebration for us; we are convinced, in fact, that God is always everywhere. We sing while we work...we pray while we carry out all life's other occupations.

St. Clement of Alexandria

A PATTERN OF GOOD WORKS

In all things showing yourself to be a pattern of good works; in doctrine showing integrity, reverence, incorruptibility . . . .

Titus 2:7 NKJV

It has been said that character is what we are when nobody is watching. How true. But, as Bill Hybels correctly observed, "Every secret act of character, conviction, and courage has been observed in living color by our omniscient God." And isn't that a sobering thought?

When we do things that we know aren't right, we try to hide our misdeeds from family members and friends. But even then, God is watching.

If you sincerely wish to walk with God, you must seek, to the best of your ability, to follow His commandments. When you do, your character will take care of itself . . . and you won't need to look over your shoulder to see who, besides God, is watching.

Let God use times of waiting to mold and shape your character. Let God use those times to purify you life and make you into a clean vessel for His service.

Henry Blackaby and Claude King

CHRIST'S LOVE CHANGES EVERYTHING

Your old life is dead. Your new life, which is your real life—even though invisible to spectators—is with Christ in God. He is your life.

Colossians 3:3 MSG

What does the love of Christ mean to His believers? It changes everything. His love is perfect and steadfast. Even though we are fallible, and wayward, the Good Shepherd cares for us still. Even though we have fallen far short of the Father's commandments, Christ loves us with a power and depth that is beyond our understanding. And, as we accept Christ's love and walk in Christ's footsteps, our lives bear testimony to His power and to His grace. Yes, Christ's love changes everything; may we invite Him into our hearts so it can then change everything in us.

No man ever loved like Jesus. He taught the blind to see and the dumb to speak. He died on the cross to save us. He bore our sins. And now God says, "Because He did, I can forgive you."

Billy Graham

NOT ENOUGH TIME?

It is good to give thanks to the LORD, to sing praises to the Most High. It is good to proclaim your unfailing love in the morning, your faithfulness in the evening.

Psalm 92:1-2 NLT

Each day has 1,440 minutes—do you value your relationship with God enough to spend a few of those minutes with Him? He deserves that much of your time and more—is He receiving it from you? Hopefully so. But if you find that you're simply "too busy" for a daily chat with your Father in heaven, it's time to take a long, hard look at your priorities and your values.

As you consider your plans for the day ahead, here's a tip. Organize your life around this simple principle: "God first." When you place your Creator where He belongs—at the very center of your day and your life—the rest of your priorities will fall into place.

Meditating upon His Word will inevitably bring peace of mind, strength of purpose, and power for living.

Bill Bright

TAKING UP THE CROSS

Then He said to them all, "If anyone wants to come with Me, he must deny himself, take up his cross daily, and follow Me."

Luke 9:23 HCSB

When we have been saved by Christ, we can, if we choose, become passive Christians. We can sit back, secure in our own salvation, and let other believers spread the healing message of Jesus. But to do so is wrong. Instead, we are commanded to become disciples of the One who has saved us, and to do otherwise is a sin of omission with terrible consequences.

When Jesus addressed His disciples, He warned them that each one must, "take up his cross daily and follow me" (Luke 9:23 NIV). Christ's message was clear: in order to follow Him, Christ's disciples must deny themselves and, instead, trust Him completely. Nothing has changed since then.

Do you seek to fulfill God's purpose for your life? Then follow Christ. Follow Him by picking up His cross today and every day that you live. Then, you will quickly discover that Christ's love has the power to change everything, including you.

TODAY'S OPPORTUNITIES

But encourage each other daily, while it is still called today, so that none of you is hardened by sin's deception.

Hebrews 3:13 HCSB

The 118th Psalm reminds us, "This is the day which the LORD hath made; we will rejoice and be glad in it" (v. 24 KJV). As we rejoice in this day that the Lord has given us, let us remember that an important part of today's celebration is the time we spend celebrating others. Each day provides countless opportunities to encourage others and to praise their good works. When we do, we not only spread seeds of joy and happiness; we also follow the commandments of the Bible.

How can we build others up? By celebrating their victories and their accomplishments. So look for the good in others and celebrate the good that you find. When you do, you'll be a powerful force of encouragement in the world . . . and a worthy servant to your God.

Those who keep speaking about the sun while walking under a cloudy sky are messengers of hope, the true saints of our day.

Henri J. Nouwen

CONTAGIOUS FAITH

Whatever you do, work at it with all your heart, as working for the Lord, not for men.

Colossians 3:23 NIV

Genuine, heartfelt Christianity is contagious. If you enjoy a life-altering relationship with God, that relationship will have an impact on others—perhaps a profound impact.

Are you genuinely excited about your faith? And do you make your enthusiasm known to those around you? Or are you a "silent ambassador" for Christ? God's preference is clear: He intends that you stand before others and proclaim your faith.

Does Christ reign over your life? Then share your testimony and your excitement. The world needs both.

There seems to be a chilling fear of holy enthusiasm among the people of God. We try to tell how happy we are—but we remain so well-controlled that there are very few waves of glory experienced in our midst.

A. W. Tozer

Sour godliness is the devil's religion.

John Wesley

IN HIS HANDS

For whatever is born of God overcomes the world. And this is the victory that has overcome the world—our faith.

1 John 5:4 NKJV

The first element of a successful life is faith: faith in God, faith in His Son, and faith in His promises. If we place our lives in God's hands, our faith is rewarded in ways that we—as human beings with clouded vision and limited understanding—can scarcely comprehend. But, if we seek to rely solely upon our own resources, or if we seek earthly success outside the boundaries of God's commandments, we reap a bitter harvest for ourselves and for our loved ones.

Do you desire the abundance and success that God has promised? Then trust Him today and every day that you live. Then, when you have entrusted your future to the Giver of all things good, rest assured that your future is secure, not only for today, but also for all eternity.

The Christian life is one of faith, where we find ourselves routinely overdriving our headlights but knowing it's okay because God is in control and has a purpose behind it.

Bill Hybels

CALMING YOUR FEARS

Be not afraid; only believe.

Mark 5:36 NKJV

Most of the things we worry about will never come to pass, yet we worry still. We worry about the future and the past; we worry about finances and relationships. As we survey the landscape of our lives, we observe all manner of molehills and imagine them to be mountains.

Are you concerned about the inevitable challenges that make up the fabric of everyday life? If so, why not ask God to help you regain a clear perspective about the problems (and opportunities) that confront you? When you petition your Heavenly Father sincerely and seek His guidance, He can touch your heart, clear your vision, renew your mind, and calm your fears.

God alone can give us songs in the night.

C. H. *Spurgeon*

Fear lurks in the shadows of every area of life. The future may look very threatening. Jesus says, "Stop being afraid. Trust me!"

Charles Swindoll

IN FOCUS

Look straight ahead, and fix your eyes on what lies before you. Mark out a straight path for your feet; then stick to the path and stay safe. Don't get sidetracked; keep your feet from following evil.

Proverbs 4:25-27 NLT

What is your focus today? Are you willing to focus your thoughts and energies on God's blessings and upon His will for your life? Or will you turn your thoughts to other things? This day—and every day hereafter—is a chance to celebrate the life that God has given you. It's also a chance to give thanks to the One who has offered you more blessings than you can possibly count.

Today, why not focus your thoughts on the joy that is rightfully yours in Christ? Why not take time to celebrate God's glorious creation? Why not trust your hopes instead of your fears? When you do, you will think optimistically about yourself and your world . . . and you can then share your optimism with others. They'll be better for it, and so will you. But not necessarily in that order.

GOD'S NEVER-ENDING FORGIVENESS

If we confess our sins, he is faithful and just and will forgive us our sins and purify us from all unrighteousness.

1 John 1:9 NIV

The Bible promises you this: When you ask God for forgiveness, He will give it. No questions asked; no explanations required.

God's power to forgive, like His love, is infinite. Despite your sins, God offers immediate forgiveness. And it's time to take Him up on His offer.

When it comes to forgiveness, God doesn't play favorites and neither should you. You should forgive all the people who have harmed you (not just the people who have asked for forgiveness or the ones who have made restitution). Complete forgiveness is God's way, and it should be your way, too. Anything less is not enough.

The sequence of forgiveness and then repentance, rather than repentance and then forgiveness, is crucial for understanding the gospel of grace.

Brennan Manning

EXCUSES AND MORE EXCUSES

And now, children, stay with Christ. Live deeply in Christ. Then we'll be ready for him when he appears, ready to receive him with open arms, with no cause for red-faced guilt or lame excuses when he arrives.

1 John 2:28-29 MSG

We live in a world where excuses are everywhere. And it's precisely because excuses are so numerous that they are also so ineffective. When we hear the words, "I'm sorry but . . . ," most of us know exactly what is to follow: the excuse. The dog ate the homework. Traffic was terrible. It's the company's fault. The boss is to blame. The equipment is broken. We're out of that. And so forth, and so on.

Because we humans are such creative excuse-makers, all of the really good excuses have already been taken. In fact, the high-quality excuses have been used, re-used, over-used, and ab-used. That's why excuses don't work—we've heard them all before.

So, if you're wasting your time trying to concoct a new and improved excuse, don't bother. It's impossible. A far better strategy is this: do the work. Now. And let your excellent work speak loudly and convincingly for itself.

QUALITY TIME

So teach us to number our days, that we may gain a heart of wisdom.

Psalm 90:12 NKJV

Make no mistake: caring for your family requires time—lots of time. You've probably heard about "quality time" and "quantity time." Your family needs both. So, as a responsible Christian, you should willingly invest large quantities of your time and energy in the care and nurturing of your clan.

While caring for your family, you should do your best to ensure that God remains squarely at the center of your household. When you do, God will bless you and yours in ways that you could have scarcely imagined.

Never give your family the leftovers and crumbs of your time.

Charles Swindoll

Overcommitment and time pressures are the greatest destroyers of marriages and families. It takes time to develop any friendship, whether with a loved one or with God himself.

James Dobson

YOUR BODY, GOD'S TEMPLE

Don't you know that you are God's temple and that God's Spirit lives in you?

1 Corinthians 3:16 NCV

Physical fitness requires discipline: the discipline to exercise regularly and the discipline to eat sensibly—it's as simple as that. But here's the catch: understanding the need for discipline is easy, but leading a disciplined life can be hard for most of us. Why? Because it's usually more fun to eat a second piece of cake than it is to jog a second lap around the track. But, as we survey the second helpings that all too often find their way on to our plates, we should consider this: when we behave in undisciplined ways, we suffer.

Are you choosing to treat your body like a temple? Hopefully so because physical fitness is a choice—a choice that determines how well you live and how long you live. So treat your body like a one-of-a-kind gift from God . . . because that's precisely what your body is.

Maximum physical health happens when the body—with all its chemicals, parts, and systems—is functioning as closely to the way God designed it to function.

Dr. Walt Larimore

INFINITE FORGIVENESS

And forgive us our sins, for we ourselves also forgive everyone in debt to us.

Luke 11:4 NKJV

God's power to forgive, like His love, is infinite. Despite your shortcomings, despite your sins, God offers you immediate forgiveness and eternal life when you accept Christ as your Savior.

As a believer who is the recipient of God's forgiveness, how should you behave toward others? Should you forgive them (just as God has forgiven you), or should you remain embittered and resentful? The answer, of course, is found in God's Word: you are instructed to forgive others. When you do, you not only obey God's command; you also free yourself from a prison of your own making.

Because God has carried the cost of human sin, you do not need to bear either the burden of your own sin or the pain of the injuries you have received from others.

Stanley Grenz

ETERNAL PERSPECTIVE

Our Savior Jesus poured out new life so generously. God's gift has restored our relationship with him and given us back our lives. And there's more life to come—an eternity of life!

Titus 3:6-7 MSG

As mere mortals, our vision for the future, like our lives here on earth, is limited. God's vision is not burdened by such limitations: His plans extend throughout all eternity. Thus, God's plans for you are not limited to the ups and downs of everyday life. Your Heavenly Father has bigger things in mind . . . much bigger things.

Christ sacrificed His life on the cross so that we might have eternal life. This gift, freely given by God's only begotten Son, is the priceless possession of everyone who accepts Him as Lord and Savior. So, when you encounter troubles, keep things in perspective. Although you will experience occasional defeats in this world, you'll have all eternity to celebrate the ultimate victory in the next.

We should live in light of being called out of this world at any time into the presence of God, where we will receive our eternal reward.

John MacArthur

SHARING YOUR FAITH

This and this only has been my appointed work: getting this news to those who have never heard of God, and explaining how it works by simple faith and plain truth.

1 Timothy 2:7 MSG

Genuine faith is never meant to be locked up in the heart of a believer; to the contrary, it is meant to be shared with the world. But, if you sincerely seek to share your faith, you must first find it.

When a suffering woman sought healing by merely touching the hem of His cloak, Jesus replied, "Daughter, be of good comfort; thy faith hath made thee whole" (Matthew 9:22 KJV). The message to believers of every generation is clear: live by faith today and every day.

How can you strengthen your faith? Through praise, through worship, through Bible study, and through prayer. And, as your faith becomes stronger, you will find ways to share it with your friends, your family, and with the world.

Our faith grows by expression. If we want to keep our faith, we must share it. We must act.

Billy Graham

INVESTING IN FELLOWSHIP

How good and pleasant it is when brothers live together in unity!

Psalm 133:1 NIV

Fellowship with other believers should be an integral part of your everyday life. Your association with fellow Christians should be uplifting, enlightening, encouraging, and consistent.

Are you an active member of your own fellowship? Are you a builder of bridges inside the four walls of your church and outside it? Do you contribute to God's glory by contributing your time and your talents to a close-knit band of believers? Hopefully so. The fellowship of believers is intended to be a powerful tool for spreading God's Good News and uplifting His children. And God intends for you to be a fully contributing member of that fellowship. Your intentions should be the same.

One cannot arrive at and maintain individual conviction of faith in isolation from the already existing community of faith.

Albrecht Ritschl

EXTREME CHANGES

Then He said to them all, "If anyone wants to come with Me, he must deny himself, take up his cross daily, and follow Me."

Luke 9:23 HCSB

Jesus made an extreme sacrifice for you. Are you willing to make extreme changes in your life for Him? Can you honestly say that you're passionate about your faith and that you're really following Jesus? Hopefully so. But if you're preoccupied with other things—or if you're strictly a one-day-a-week Christian—then you're in need of an extreme spiritual makeover!

Nothing is more important than your wholehearted commitment to your Creator and to His only Son. Your faith must never be an afterthought; it must be your ultimate priority, your ultimate possession, and your ultimate passion. You are the recipient of Christ's love. Accept it enthusiastically and share it passionately. Jesus deserves your extreme enthusiasm; the world deserves it; and you deserve the experience of sharing it.

You will never change your life until you change something you do daily.

John Maxwell

HONORING GOD WITH THE COMPANY YOU KEEP

If your life honors the name of Jesus, he will honor you.

2 Thessalonians 1:12 MSG

Some friendships help us honor God; these friendships should be nurtured. Other friendships place us in situations where we are tempted to dishonor God by disobeying His commandments; friendships such as these have the potential to do us great harm.

Because we tend to become like our friends, we must choose our friends carefully. Because our friends influence us in ways that are both subtle and powerful, we must ensure that our friendships are pleasing to God. When we spend our days in the presence of godly believers, we are blessed, not only by those friends, but also by our Creator.

I have found that the closer I am to the godly people around me, the easier it is for me to live a righteous life because they hold me accountable.

John MacArthur

In a circle of true friends each man is simply what he is: stands for nothing but himself.

C. S. Lewis

THE PLACE HE DESERVES

You shall have no other gods before Me.

Exodus 20:3 NKJV

When Jesus was tempted by Satan, the Master's response was unambiguous. Jesus chose to worship God and serve Him only. We, as followers of Christ, must follow in His footsteps by placing God first.

When we place God in a position of secondary importance, we do ourselves great harm. When we allow temptations or distractions to come between us and our Creator, we suffer. But, when we imitate Jesus and place the Lord in His rightful place—at the center of our lives—then we claim spiritual treasures that will endure forever.

There is a God shaped vacuum in the heart of every man which cannot be filled by any created thing, but only by God, the Creator, made known through Jesus.

Blaise Pascal

GOD'S GUIDANCE

The steps of the Godly are directed by God. He delights in every detail of their lives.

Psalm 37:22 NLT

God is intensely interested in each of us, and He will guide our steps if we serve Him obediently.

When we sincerely offer heartfelt prayers to our Heavenly Father, He will give direction and meaning to our lives—but He won't force us to follow Him. To the contrary, God has given us the free will to follow His commandments . . . or not.

When we stray from God's commandments, we invite bitter consequences. But, when we follow His commandments, and when we genuinely and humbly seek His will, He touches our hearts and leads us on the path of His choosing.

Will you trust God to guide your steps? You should. When you entrust your life to Him completely and without reservation, God will give you the strength to meet any challenge, the courage to face any trial, and the wisdom to live in His righteousness and in His peace. So trust Him today and seek His guidance. When you do, your next step will be the right one.

HIS PROMISES

Let's keep a firm grip on the promises that keep us going. He always keeps his word.

Hebrews 10:23 MSG

The Christian faith is founded upon promises that are contained in a unique book. That book is the Holy Bible. The Bible is a roadmap for life here on earth and for life eternal. As Christians, we are called upon to study its meaning, to trust its promises, to follow its commandments, and to share its Good News. God's Holy Word is, indeed, a transforming, life-changing, one-of-a-kind treasure. And, a passing acquaintance with the Good Book is insufficient for Christians who seek to obey God's Word and understand His will.

God has made promises to you, and He intends to keep them. So take God at His word: trust His promises and share them with your family, with your friends, and with the world.

There is a living God; he has spoken in the Bible. He means what he says and will do all he has promised.

Hudson Taylor

BEYOND THE SHAME

There is therefore now no condemnation to those who are in Christ Jesus, who do not walk according to the flesh, but according to the Spirit.

Romans 8:1 NKJV

All of us have sinned. Sometimes our sins result from our own stubborn rebellion against God's commandments. And sometimes, we are swept up in events that are beyond our abilities to control. Under either set of circumstances, we may experience intense feelings of guilt. But God has an answer for the guilt that we feel. That answer, of course, is His forgiveness. When we confess our wrongdoings and repent from them, we are forgiven by the One who created us.

Are you troubled by feelings of guilt or regret? If so, you must repent from your misdeeds, and you must ask your Heavenly Father for His forgiveness. When you do so, He will forgive you completely and without reservation. Then, you must forgive yourself just as God has forgiven you: thoroughly and unconditionally.

You never lose the love of God. Guilt is the warning that temporarily you are out of touch.

Jack Dominian

SEEKING GOD AND FINDING HAPPINESS

But happy are those . . . whose hope is in the L*ORD their God.*

Psalm 146:5 NLT

Happiness depends less upon our circumstances than upon our thoughts. When we turn our thoughts to God, to His gifts, and to His glorious creation, we experience the joy that God intends for His children. But, when we focus on the negative aspects of life, we suffer needlessly.

Do you sincerely want to be a happy Christian? Then set your mind and your heart upon God's love and His grace. The fullness of life in Christ is available to all who seek it and claim it. Count yourself among that number. Seek first the salvation that is available through a personal relationship with Jesus Christ, and then claim the joy, the peace, and the spiritual abundance that the Shepherd offers His sheep.

God has charged Himself with full responsibility for our eternal happiness and stands ready to take over the management of our lives the moment we turn in faith to Him.

A. W. Tozer

THE SELF-FULFILLING PROPHECY

May He grant you according to your heart's desire, and fulfill all your purpose.

Psalm 20:4 NKJV

The self-fulfilling prophecy is alive, well, and living at your house. If you trust God and have faith for the future, your optimistic beliefs will give you direction and motivation. That's one reason that you should never lose hope, but certainly not the only reason. The primary reason that you, as a believer, should never lose hope is because of God's unfailing promises.

Make no mistake about it: thoughts are powerful things; your thoughts have the power to lift you up or to hold you down. When you acquire the habit of hopeful thinking, you will have acquired a powerful tool for improving your life. So if you fall into the habit of negative thinking, think again. After all, God's Word teaches us that Christ can overcome every difficulty (John 16:33). And when God makes a promise, He keeps it.

Christ has turned all our sunsets into dawn.

St. Clement of Alexandria

COMPASSIONATE CHRISTIANITY

So, as those who have been chosen of God, holy and beloved, put on a heart of compassion, kindness, humility, gentleness and patience.

Colossians 3:12 NASB

The instructions from Colossians 3:12 are unambiguous: as Christians, we are to be compassionate, humble, gentle, and kind. But sometimes, we fall short. In the busyness of daily life, we may neglect to share a kind word or a kind deed. This oversight hurts others, but it hurts us most of all.

Today, slow yourself down and be alert for those who need your smile, your kind words, or your helping hand. Make kindness a centerpiece of your dealings with others. They will be blessed, and you will be too. Today, honor Christ by obeying His Golden Rule. He deserves no less, and neither, for that matter, do your friends.

Reach out and care for someone who needs the touch of hospitality. The time you spend caring today will be a love gift that will blossom into the fresh joy of God's Spirit in the future.

Emilie Barnes

READY. SET. GO!

Do not neglect the spiritual gift that is within you . . . .

1 Timothy 4:14 NASB

God has given you talents and opportunities that are uniquely yours. Are you willing to use your gifts in the way that God intends? And are you willing to summon the discipline that is required to develop your talents and to hone your skills? That's precisely what God wants you to do, and that's precisely what you should desire for yourself.

As you seek to expand your talents, you will undoubtedly encounter stumbling blocks along the way, such as the fear of rejection or the fear of failure. When you do, don't stumble! Just continue to refine your skills, and offer your services to God. And when the time is right, He will use you—but it's up to you to be thoroughly prepared when He does.

There's a unique sense of fulfillment that comes when we submit our gifts to God's use and ask him to energize them in a supernatural way—and then step back to watch what he does.

Lee Strobel

GREAT IS THY FAITHFULNESS

God is faithful, by whom you were called into the fellowship of His Son, Jesus Christ our Lord.

1 Corinthians 1:9 NKJV

God is faithful to us even when we are not faithful to Him. God keeps His promises to us even when we stray far from His will. He continues to love us even when we disobey His commandments. But God does not force His blessings upon us. If we are to experience His love and His grace, we must claim them for ourselves.

Are you tired, discouraged, or fearful? Be comforted: God is with you. Are you confused? Listen to the quiet voice of your Heavenly Father. Are you bitter? Talk with God and seek His guidance. Are you celebrating a great victory? Thank God and praise Him. He is the Giver of all things good. In whatever condition you find yourself, trust God and be comforted. The Father is with you now and forever.

God's faithfulness has never depended on the faithfulness of his children . . . . God is greater than our weakness. In fact, I think, it is our weakness that reveals how great God is.

Max Lucado

WITH YOU ALWAYS

You will show me the way of life, granting me the joy of your presence and the pleasures of living with you forever.

Psalm 16:11 NLT

Do you ever wonder if God is really here? If so, you're not the first person to think such thoughts. In fact, some of the biggest heroes in the Bible had their doubts—and so, perhaps, will you. But when questions arise and doubts begin to creep into your mind, remember this: You can talk with God any time. In fact, He's right here, right now, listening to your thoughts and prayers, watching over your every move.

Sometimes, you will allow yourself to become very busy, and that's when you may be tempted to ignore God. But, when you quiet yourself long enough to acknowledge His presence, God will touch your heart and restore your spirits. By the way, He's ready to talk right now. Are you?

When we are in the presence of God, removed from distractions, we are able to hear him more clearly, and a secure environment has been established for the young and broken places in our hearts to surface.

John Eldredge

SUFFICIENT FOR YOUR NEEDS

And God is able to make all grace abound toward you, that you, always having all sufficiency in all things, may have an abundance for every good work.

2 Corinthians 9:8 NKJV

Of this you can be sure: the love of God is sufficient to meet your needs. Whatever dangers you may face, whatever heartbreaks you must endure, God is with you, and He stands ready to comfort you and to heal you.

The Psalmist writes, "Weeping may endure for a night, but joy comes in the morning" (Psalm 30:5 NKJV). But when we are suffering, the morning may seem very far away. It is not. God promises that He is "near to those who have a broken heart" (Psalm 34:18 NKJV).

If you are experiencing the intense pain of a recent loss, or if you are still mourning a loss from long ago, perhaps you are now ready to begin the next stage of your journey with God. If so, be mindful of this fact: the loving heart of God is sufficient to meet any challenge, including yours.

The grace of God is sufficient for all our needs, for every problem and for every difficulty, for every broken heart, and for every human sorrow.

Peter Marshall

AN ATTITUDE OF GRATITUDE

And let the peace of God rule in your hearts . . . and be ye thankful.

Colossians 3:15 KJV

For most of us, life is busy and complicated. We have countless responsibilities, some of which begin before sunrise and many of which end long after sunset. Amid the rush and crush of the daily grind, it is easy to lose sight of God and His blessings. But, when we forget to slow down and say "Thank You" to our Maker, we rob ourselves of His presence, His peace, and His joy.

Our task, as believing Christians, is to praise God many times each day. Then, with gratitude in our hearts, we can face our daily duties with the perspective and power that only He can provide.

It is only with gratitude that life becomes rich.

Dietrich Bonhoeffer

No duty is more urgent than that of returning thanks.

St. Ambrose

FILLED WITH THE SPIRIT

Do not be drunk with wine, which will ruin you, but be filled with the Spirit.

Ephesians 5:18 NCV

When you are filled with the Holy Spirit, your words and deeds will reflect a love and devotion to Christ. When you are filled with the Holy Spirit, the steps of your life's journey are guided by the Lord. When you allow God's Spirit to work in you and through you, you will be energized and transformed.

Today, allow yourself to be filled with the Spirit of God. And then stand back in amazement as God begins to work miracles in your own life and in the lives of those you love.

Whether we preach, pray, write, do business, travel, take care of children, or administer the government—whatever we do—our whole life and influence should be filled with the power of the Holy Spirit.

Charles Finney

God cannot reveal anything to us if we have not His spirit.

Oswald Chambers

HOPE FOR TODAY

The lines of purpose in your lives never grow slack, tightly tied as they are to your future in heaven, kept taut by hope.

Colossians 1:5 MSG

The hope that the world offers is fleeting and imperfect. The hope that God offers is unchanging, unshakable, and unending. It is no wonder, then, that when we seek security from worldly sources, our are hopes are often dashed. Thankfully, God has no such record of failure.

Where will you place your hopes today? Will you entrust your future to man or to God? Will you seek solace exclusively from fallible human beings, or will you place your hopes, first and foremost, in the trusting hands of your Creator? The decision is yours, and you must live with the results of the choices you make.

For thoughtful believers, hope begins with God. Period. So today, as you embark upon the next stage of your life's journey, consider the words of the Psalmist: "You are my hope; O Lord GOD, You are my confidence" (71:5 NASB). Then, place your trust in the One who cannot be shaken.

A SHINING LIGHT

While ye have light, believe in the light, that ye may be the children of light.

John 12:36 KJV

God's Holy Word instructs us that Jesus is, "the way, the truth, and the life" (John 14:6-7). Without Christ, we are as far removed from salvation as the east is removed from the west. And without Christ, we can never know the ultimate truth: God's truth.

Truth is God's way: He commands His believers live in truth, and He rewards those who do so. Jesus is the personification of God's liberating truth, a truth that offers salvation to mankind.

Do you seek to walk with God? Do you seek to feel His presence and His peace? Then you must walk in truth; you must walk in the light; you must walk with the Savior. There is simply no other way.

May all my life be filled by the radiance of Thy presence. Let the Spirit of Him whose life was the light of men rule within my heart till eventide.

John Baillie

THE MIRACLE WORKER

Jesus said to them, "I have shown you many great miracles from the Father."

John 10:32 NIV

God is a miracle worker. Throughout history He has intervened in the course of human events in ways that cannot be explained by science or human rationale. And He's still doing so today.

God's miracles are not limited to special occasions, nor are they witnessed by a select few. God is crafting His wonders all around us: the miracle of the birth of a baby; the miracle of a world renewing itself with every sunrise; the miracle of lives transformed by God's love and grace. Each day, God's handiwork is evident for all to see and experience.

Today, seize the opportunity to inspect God's hand at work. His miracles come in a variety of shapes and sizes, so keep your eyes and your heart open. Be watchful, and you'll soon be amazed.

Too many times we miss so much because we live on the low level of the natural, the ordinary, the explainable.

Vance Havner

A PASSIONATE LIFE

Never be lacking in zeal, but keep your spiritual fervor, serving the Lord.

Romans 12:11 NIV

Are you passionate about your life, your loved ones, your work, and your faith? As a believer who has been saved by a risen Christ, you should be.

As a thoughtful Christian, you have every reason to be enthusiastic about life, but sometimes the inevitable struggles of life may cause you to feel decidedly unenthusiastic. If you feel that your enthusiasm is slowly fading away, it's time to slow down, to rest, to count your blessings, and to pray. When you feel worried or weary, you must pray fervently for God to renew your sense of wonderment and excitement.

Life with God is a glorious adventure; revel in it. When you do, God will most certainly smile upon your work and your life.

But what hope have we if, while singing "Onward Christian Soldiers," we go through perfunctory services, parroting prayers, yawning over watches, acting as if we were excursionists on a pleasure expedition?

R. G. Lee

THE SOURCE OF ALL COMFORT

When doubts filled my mind, your comfort gave me renewed hope and cheer.

Psalm 94:19 NLT

In times of adversity, we are wise to remember the words of Jesus, who, when He walked on the waters, reassured His disciples, saying, "Take courage! It is I. Don't be afraid" (Matthew 14:27 NIV). Then, with Christ on His throne—and with trusted friends and loving family members at our sides—we can face our fears with courage and with faith.

Are you facing a difficult challenge? If so, remember that no problem is too big for God . . . not even yours.

Discouraged people don't need critics. They hurt enough already. They don't need more guilt or piled-on distress. They need encouragement. They need a refuge, a willing, caring, available someone.

Charles Swindoll

GOD'S VOICE

For this is commendable, if because of conscience toward God one endures grief, suffering wrongfully.

1 Peter 2:19 NKJV

Billy Graham correctly observed, "Most of us follow our conscience as we follow a wheelbarrow. We push it in front of us in the direction we want to go." To do so, of course, is a profound mistake. Yet all of us, on occasion, have failed to listen to the voice that God planted in our hearts, and all of us have suffered the consequences.

God gave you a conscience for a very good reason: to make your path conform to His will. Wise believers make it a practice to listen carefully to that quiet internal voice. Count yourself among that number. When your conscience speaks, listen and learn. In all likelihood, God is trying to get His message through. And in all likelihood, it is a message that you desperately need to hear.

Many words do not satisfy the soul; but a good life eases the mind and a clean conscience inspires great trust in God.

Thomas à Kempis

MOUNTAINTOPS AND VALLEYS

I sought the LORD, *and he answered me; he delivered me from all my fears.*

Psalm 34:4 NIV

Every life (including yours) is an unfolding series of events: some fabulous, some not-so-fabulous, and some downright disheartening. When you reach the mountaintops of life, praising God is easy. But, when the storm clouds form overhead, your faith will be tested, sometimes to the breaking point. As a believer, you can take comfort in this fact: Wherever you find yourself, whether at the top of the mountain or the depths of the valley, God is there, and because He cares for you, you can live courageously.

The next time you find your courage tested to the limit, remember that God is your shield and your strength; He is your protector and your deliverer. Call upon Him in your hour of need and He will protect you.

Feelings of uselessness and hopelessness are not from God, but from the evil one, the devil, who wants to discourage you and thwart your effectiveness for the Lord.

Bill Bright

MAKING WISE DECISIONS

An indecisive man is unstable in all his ways.

James 1:8 HCSB

From the instant you wake in the morning until the moment you nod off to sleep at night, you have the opportunity to make countless decisions: decisions about the things you do, decisions about the words you speak, and decisions about the thoughts you choose to think.

If you're facing one of life's major decisions, here are some things you can do: 1. Gather as much information as you can. 2. Don't be too impulsive. 3. Rely on the advice of trusted friends and mentors. 4. Pray for guidance. 5. Trust the quiet inner voice of your conscience. 6. When the time for action arrives, act. Procrastination is the enemy of progress; don't let it defeat you.

People who can never quite seem to make up their minds usually make themselves miserable. So when in doubt, be decisive. It's the decent way to live.

You should not believe your conscience and your feelings more than the word which the Lord who receives sinners preaches to you.

Martin Luther

FINDING ENCOURAGEMENT

Be strong and courageous. Do not be terrified; do not be discouraged, for the LORD your God will be with you wherever you go.

Joshua 1:9 NIV

When we fail to meet the expectations of others (or, for that matter, the expectations that we have set for ourselves), we may be tempted to abandon hope. Thankfully, on those cloudy days when our strength is sapped and our faith is shaken, there exists a source from which we can draw courage and wisdom. That source is God.

When we seek to form a more intimate and dynamic relationship with our Creator, He renews our spirits and restores our souls. God's promise is made clear in Isaiah 40:31: "But those who wait on the Lord shall renew their strength; They shall mount up with wings like eagles, They shall run and not be weary, They shall walk and not faint" (NKJV). And upon this promise we can—and should—depend.

It is impossible for that man to despair who remembers that his helper is omnipotent.

Jeremy Taylor

ENERGIZED FOR LIFE

Be energetic in your life of salvation, reverent and sensitive before God. That energy is God's energy, an energy deep within you, God himself willing and working at what will give him the most pleasure.

Philippians 2:12-13 MSG

Are you fired up with enthusiasm for Christ? If so, congratulations, and keep up the good work! But, if your spiritual batteries are running low, then perhaps you're spending too much energy working for yourself and not enough energy working for God.

If you're feeling tired or troubled, or both, don't despair. Instead, seek strength from the source that never fails; that source, of course, is your Heavenly Father. And rest assured—when you sincerely petition Him, He will give you all the strength you need to live victoriously for Him.

God doesn't camouflage the old; he restores the new. The Master Builder will pull out the original plan and restore it. He will restore the vigor, he will restore the energy. He will restore the hope. He will restore the soul.

Max Lucado

PERFECT WISDOM

Therefore everyone who hears these words of mine and puts them into practice is like a wise man who built his house on the rock.

Matthew 7:24-25 NIV

Where will you place your trust today? Will you trust in the wisdom of fallible men and women, or will you place your faith in God's perfect wisdom? Where you choose to place your trust will determine the direction and quality of your life.

Are you tired? Discouraged? Fearful? Be comforted and trust God. Are you worried or anxious? Be confident in God's power and trust His Holy Word. Are you confused? Listen to the quiet voice of your Heavenly Father. He is not a God of confusion. Talk with Him; listen to Him; trust Him. He is steadfast, and He is your protector . . . forever.

The Spirit of God is direct, authoritative, the foundation of wisdom, life, and holiness.

St. John of Damascus

If you lack knowledge, go to school. If you lack wisdom, get on your knees.

Vance Havner

CHOOSING WISELY

I shall yet praise him, who is the health of my countenance, and my God.

Psalm 42:11 KJV

The journey toward improved health is not only a common-sense exercise in personal discipline; it is also a spiritual journey ordained by God. He does not intend that we abuse our bodies by giving in to excessive appetites or to slothful behavior. To the contrary, He has instructed us to protect our physical bodies to the greatest extent we can. To do otherwise is to disobey Him.

God's plan for you includes provisions for your spiritual, physical, and emotional health. But, He expects you to do your fair share of the work! In a world that is full of temptations, you may find it all too easy to make unhealthy choices. Your challenge, of course, is to resist those unhealthy temptations by every means you can, including prayer. And rest assured: when you ask for God's help, He will give it.

People are funny. When they are young, they will spend their health to get wealth. Later, they will gladly pay all they have trying to get their health back.

John Maxwell

SHOUTING THE GOOD NEWS

As you go, preach this message: "The kingdom of heaven is near."

Matthew 10:7 NIV

The Good News of Jesus Christ should be shouted from the rooftops by believers the world over. But all too often, it is not. For a variety of reasons, many Christians keep their beliefs to themselves, and when they do, the world suffers because of their failure to speak up.

As believers, we are called to share the transforming message of Jesus with our families, with our neighbors, and with the world. Jesus commands us to become fishers of men. And, the time to go fishing is now. We must share the Good News of Jesus Christ today—tomorrow may indeed be too late.

Every tiny bit of my life that has value I owe to the redemption of Jesus Christ. Am I doing anything to enable Him to bring His redemption into evident reality in the lives of others?

Oswald Chambers

THE WISDOM TO OBEY

The world and its desires pass away, but the man who does the will of God lives forever.

1 John 2:17 NIV

Since God created Adam and Eve, we human beings have been rebelling against our Creator. Why? Because we are unwilling to trust God's Word, and we are unwilling to follow His commandments. God has given us a guidebook for righteous living called the Holy Bible. It contains thorough instructions which, if followed, lead to fulfillment, righteousness, and salvation. But, if we choose to ignore God's commandments, the results are as predictable as they are tragic.

Talking about God is easy; living by His commandments is considerably harder. But, unless we are willing to abide by God's laws, all of our righteous proclamations ring hollow. How can we best proclaim our love for the Lord? By obeying Him. And, for further instructions, read the manual.

Obedience is the key of knowledge.

Christina Rossetti

GOOD PRESSURES, BAD PRESSURES

Do you think I am trying to make people accept me? No, God is the One I am trying to please. Am I trying to please people? If I still wanted to please people, I would not be a servant of Christ.

Galatians 1:10 NCV

Our world is filled with pressures: some good, some bad. The pressures that we feel to follow God's will and obey His commandments are positive pressures. God places them on our hearts, and He intends that we act in accordance with His leadings. But we also face different pressures, ones that are definitely not from God. When we feel pressured to do things—or even to think thoughts—that lead us away from God, we must beware.

Society seeks to mold us into more worldly beings; God seeks to mold us into new beings that are most certainly not conformed to this world. If we are to please God, we must resist the pressures that society seeks to impose upon us, and we must conform ourselves, instead, to God's will, to His path, and to His Son.

NO IS AN ANSWER

God answered their prayers because they trusted him.

1 Chronicles 5:20 MSG

God answers our prayers. What God does not do is this: He does not always answer our prayers as soon as we might like, and He does not always answer our prayers by saying "Yes." God isn't an order-taker, and He's not some sort of cosmic vending machine. Sometimes—even when we want something very badly—our loving Heavenly Father responds to our requests by saying "No," and we must accept His answer, even if we don't understand it.

God answers prayers not only according to our wishes but also according to His master plan. We cannot know that plan, but we can know the Planner . . . and we must trust His wisdom, His righteousness, and His love. Always.

Prayer is request. The essence of request, as distinct from compulsion, is that it may or may not be granted. And if an infinitely wise being listens to the requests of finite and foolish creatures, of course He will sometimes grant and sometimes refuse them.

C. S. Lewis

TAKING RISKS

Is anything too hard for the LORD?

Genesis 18:14 NKJV

As we consider the uncertainties of the future, we are confronted with a powerful temptation: the temptation to "play it safe." Unwilling to move mountains, we fret over molehills. Unwilling to entertain great hopes for tomorrow, we focus on the unfairness of today. Unwilling to trust God completely, we take timid half-steps when God intends that we make giant leaps.

Today, ask God for the courage to step beyond the boundaries of your doubts. Ask Him to guide you to a place where you can realize your full potential—a place where you are freed from the fear of failure. Ask Him to do His part, and promise Him that you will do your part. Don't ask Him to lead you to a "safe" place; ask Him to lead you to the "right" place . . . and remember: those two places are seldom the same.

The really committed leave the safety of the harbor, accept the risk of the open seas of faith, and set their compasses for the place of total devotion to God and whatever life adventures He plans for them.

Bill Hybels

ABUNDANT PEACE

And the peace of God, which surpasses all comprehension, will guard your hearts and your minds in Christ Jesus.

Philippians 4:7 NASB

If you are a thoughtful believer, you will open yourself to the spiritual abundance that your Savior offers by following Him completely and without reservation. When you do, you will receive the love, the peace, and the joy that He has promised.

Do you sincerely seek the riches that our Savior offers to those who give themselves to Him? Then follow Him. When you do, you will receive the love and the abundance that He has promised. Seek first the salvation that is available through a personal, passionate relationship with Christ, and then claim the joy, the peace, and the spiritual abundance that the Shepherd offers His sheep.

God loves you and wants you to experience peace and life—abundant and eternal.

Billy Graham

STRENGTH FOR THE STRUGGLE

Now I take limitations in stride, and with good cheer, these limitations that cut me down to size—abuse, accidents, opposition, bad breaks. I just let Christ take over! And so the weaker I get, the stronger I become.

2 Corinthians 12:10 MSG

Life is a tapestry of good days and difficult days, with good days predominating. During the good days, we are tempted to take our blessings for granted (a temptation that we must resist with all our might). But, during life's difficult and trying days, we discover precisely what we're made of. And more importantly, we discover what our faith is made of.

Has your faith been put to the test yet? If so, then you know that with God's help, you can endure life's darker days. But if you have not yet faced the inevitable trials and tragedies of life here on earth, don't worry; you will. And when your faith is put to the test, rest assured that God is perfectly willing—and always ready—to give you strength for the struggle.

THE COURAGE TO LIVE BOLDLY

God doesn't want us to be shy with his gifts, but bold and loving and sensible.

2 Timothy 1:7 MSG

Do you prefer to face your fears rather than run from them? If so, you will be blessed because of your willingness to live courageously.

When Paul wrote Timothy, he reminded his young protégé that the God they served was a bold God, and God's Spirit empowered His children with boldness also. Like Timothy, we face times of uncertainty and fear. God's message is the same to us, today, as it was to Timothy: We can live boldly because the spirit of God resides in us.

So today, as you face the challenges of everyday living, remember that God is with you . . . and you are protected.

The Holy Spirit is no skeptic, and the things he has written in our hearts are not doubts or opinions, but assertions—surer and more certain than sense or life itself.

Martin Luther

GOD KNOWS . . . AND CARES

As for myself, I do not care if I am judged by you or by any human court. I do not even judge myself. I know of no wrong I have done, but this does not make me right before the Lord. The Lord is the One who judges me.

1 Corinthians 4:3-4 NCV

If you're like most people, you seek the admiration of your neighbors, your co-workers, and your family members. But the eagerness to please others should never overshadow your eagerness to please God. If you seek to fulfill the purposes that God has in store for you, then you must be a "doer of the Word." And how can you do so? By putting God first.

Martin Luther issued this stern warning: "You may as well quit reading and hearing the Word of God and give it to the devil if you do not desire to live according to it." Luther understood that obedience leads to abundance just as surely as disobedience leads to disaster; you should understand it, too.

Would you like a time-tested formula for successful living? Here it is: Don't just listen to God's Word; live by it. Does this sound too simple? Perhaps it is simple, but it is also the only way to reap the marvelous riches that God has in store for you.

HEEDING GOD'S CALL

One thing I do, forgetting those things which are behind and reaching forward to those things which are ahead, I press toward the goal for the prize of the upward call of God in Christ Jesus.

Philippians 3:13-14 NKJV

It is vitally important that you heed God's call. In John 15:16, Jesus says, "You did not choose me, but I chose you and appointed you to go and bear fruit—fruit that will last" (NIV). In other words, you have been called by Christ, and now, it is up to you to decide precisely how you will answer.

Have you already found your special calling? If so, you're a very lucky man. If not, keep searching and keep praying until you discover it. And remember this: God has important work for you to do—work that no one else on earth can accomplish but you.

When you become consumed by God's call on your life, everything will take on new meaning and significance. You will begin to see every facet of your life, including your pain, as a means through which God can work to bring others to Himself.

Charles Stanley

PRICELESS TREASURES

The promise is for you and your children.

Acts 2:39 NASB

Have you hugged a child lately? If so, you've experienced one of life's great pleasures. Every child is a priceless gift from the Creator. When we share love and affection with our children, we—and they—are blessed beyond measure.

As parents, friends of parents, uncles, and grandfathers, we understand the critical importance of raising our children with love, with discipline, and with God. It's a tall order and a profoundly important responsibility . . . but with God's help, we can do it.

Every child deserves the presence of caring adults who serve as godly role models. May we, as concerned adults, behave ourselves—and raise our children—accordingly.

Each child is unique, a special creation of God with talents, abilities, personality, preference, dislikes, potentials, strengths, weaknesses, and skills that are his or her own. As parents, we must seek to identify these in each of our children and help them become the persons God intended.

Dave Veerman

OUR ULTIMATE SAVIOR

And we have seen and testify that the Father has sent the Son as Savior of the world.

1 John 4:14 NKJV

Are you willing to place God first in your life? And, are you willing to welcome God's Son into your heart? Unless you can honestly answer these questions with a resounding yes, then your relationship with God isn't what it could be or should be.

As you think about the nature of your relationship with God, remember this: you will always have some type of relationship with Him—it is inevitable that your life must be lived in relationship to God. The question is not if you will have a relationship with Him; the burning question is whether or not that relationship will be one that seeks to honor Him.

Thankfully, God is always available, He's always ready to forgive, and He's waiting to hear from you now. The rest, of course, is up to you.

Christ is no Moses, no exactor, no giver of laws, but a giver of grace, a Savior; he is infinite mercy and goodness, freely and bountifully given to us.

Martin Luther

A PLACE OF WORSHIP

For where two or three come together in my name, there am I with them.

Matthew 18:20 NIV

The Bible teaches that we should worship God in our hearts and in our churches (Acts 20:28). We have clear instructions to "feed the church of God" and to worship our Creator in the presence of fellow believers.

We live in a world that is teeming with temptations and distractions—a world where good and evil struggle in a constant battle to win our minds, our hearts, and our souls. Our challenge, of course, is to ensure that we cast our lot on the side of God. One way that we remain faithful to Him is through the practice of regular, purposeful worship with our families. When we worship the Father faithfully and fervently, we are blessed.

The New Testament does not envisage solitary religion; some kind of regular assembly for worship and instruction is everywhere taken for granted in the epistles.

C. S. *Lewis*

CONTENTMENT THAT LASTS

Serving God does make us very rich, if we are satisfied with what we have. We brought nothing into the world, so we can take nothing out. But, if we have food and clothes, we will be satisfied with that.

1 Timothy 6:6-8 NCV

The preoccupation with happiness and contentment is an ever-present theme in the modern world. We are bombarded with messages that tell us where to find peace and pleasure in a world that worships materialism and wealth. But, lasting contentment is not found in material possessions; genuine contentment is a spiritual gift from God to those who trust in Him and follow His commandments. When God dwells at the center of our lives, peace and contentment will belong to us just as surely as we belong to God.

The heart is rich when it is content, and it is always content when its desires are set upon God.

St. Miguel of Ecuador

We are made for God, and nothing less will really satisfy us.

Brennan Manning

NEW AND APPROVED

If anyone belongs to Christ, there is a new creation. The old things have gone; everything is made new!

2 *Corinthians* 5:17 NCV

Think, for a moment, about the "old" you, the person you were before you invited Christ to reign over your heart. Now, think about the "new" you, the person you have become since then. Is there a difference between the "old" you and the "new and improved" version? There should be! And that difference should be noticeable not only to you but also to others.

The Bible clearly teaches that when we welcome Christ into our hearts, we become new creations through Him. Our challenge, of course, is to behave ourselves like new creations. When we do, God fills our hearts, He blesses our endeavors, and He transforms our lives . . . forever.

No man is ever the same after God has laid His hand upon him.

A. W. Tozer

ABOVE AND BEYOND OUR CIRCUMSTANCES

We take the good days from God—why not also the bad days?

Job 2:10 MSG

Sometimes the seas of life are calm, and sometimes they are not. When we find ourselves beset by the inevitable storms of life, we may sense that all is lost—but if we imagine, even for a moment, that all hope is gone, we are mistaken.

The Bible is unambiguous: it promises that God will remain steadfast, even during our darkest hours. God's Word makes it perfectly clear that He is with us always, on good days and bad days. He never leaves our side, and He never stops loving us.

So if you're feeling buffeted by the winds and the waves of life, don't despair. God is not just near; He is here. He has promised to protect you now and forever. And upon that promise, you can always depend.

God expresses His love by engineering our circumstances for our good and His glory.

Charles Stanley

DEFEATING DISCOURAGEMENT

The LORD is the One who will go before you. He will be with you; He will not leave you or forsake you. Do not be afraid or discouraged.

Deuteronomy 31:8 HCSB

Even the most devout Christians can become discouraged, and you are no exception. After all, you live in a world where expectations can be high and demands can be even higher.

If you find yourself enduring difficult circumstances, don't lose hope. If you face uncertainties about the future, don't become anxious. And if you become discouraged with the direction of your day or your life, don't despair. Instead, lift your thoughts and prayers to your Heavenly Father. He is a God of possibility, not negativity. You can be sure that He will guide you through your difficulties and beyond them . . . far beyond.

Faith and discouragement are opposites. Faith is taking God at His Word no matter how bleak the circumstances appear to be. Discouragement is focusing on distressing circumstances in spite of what God has said. Learn to trust God.

Jerry Falwell

ENTHUSIASM FOR CHRIST

So roll up your sleeves, put your mind in gear, be totally ready to receive the gift that's coming when Jesus arrives. Don't lazily slip back into those old grooves of evil, doing just what you feel like doing. You didn't know any better then; you do now.

1 Peter 1:13-15 MSG

John Wesley advised, "Catch on fire with enthusiasm and people will come for miles to watch you burn." His words still ring true. When we fan the flames of enthusiasm for Christ, our faith serves as a beacon to others.

Our world desperately needs faithful believers who share the Good News of Jesus with joyful exuberance. Be such a believer. The world desperately needs your enthusiasm—now!

We act as though comfort and luxury were the chief requirements of life, when all we need to make us really happy is something to be enthusiastic about.

Charles Kingsley

BEYOND MATERIALISM

For what will it profit a man if he gains the whole world, and loses his own soul? Or what will a man give in exchange for his soul?

Mark 8:36-37 NKJV

In our modern society, we need money to live. But as Christians, we must never make the acquisition of money the central focus of our lives. Money is a tool, but it should never overwhelm our sensibilities. The focus of life must be squarely on things spiritual, not things material.

Whenever we place our love for material possessions above our love for God—or when we yield to the countless other temptations of everyday living—we find ourselves engaged in a struggle between good and evil. Let us respond to this struggle by freeing ourselves from that subtle yet powerful temptation: the temptation to love the world more than we love God.

The socially prescribed affluent, middle-class lifestyle has become so normative in our churches that we discern little conflict between it and the Christian lifestyle prescribed in the New Testament.

Tony Compolo

GOD'S GUIDANCE AND YOUR PATH

Trust in the L*ORD* *with all your heart; do not depend on your own understanding. Seek his will in all you do, and he will direct your paths.*

Proverbs 3:5-6 NLT

Proverbs 3:5-6 makes this promise: if you acknowledge God's sovereignty over every aspect of your life, He will guide your path. And, as you prayerfully consider the path that God intends for you to take, here are things you should do: You should study His Word and be ever-watchful for His signs. You should associate with fellow believers who will encourage your spiritual growth. You should listen carefully to that inner voice that speaks to you in the quiet moments of your daily devotionals. And you should be patient. Your Heavenly Father may not always reveal Himself as quickly as you would like, but rest assured that God intends to use you in wonderful, unexpected ways. Your challenge is to watch, to listen, to learn . . . and to follow.

Only by walking with God can we hope to find the path that leads to life.

John Eldredge

WHAT KIND OF EXAMPLE?

In everything set them an example by doing what is good.

Titus 2:7 NIV

What kind of example are you? Are you the kind of man whose life serves as a powerful example of decency and morality? Are you a man whose behavior serves as a positive role model for others? Are you the kind of person whose actions, day in and day out, are based upon integrity, fidelity, and a love for the Lord? If so, you are not only blessed by God; you are also a powerful force for good in a world that desperately needs positive influences such as yours.

Phillips Brooks advised, "Be such a man, and live such a life, that if every man were such as you, and every life a life like yours, this earth would be God's Paradise." And that's sound advice because our families and friends are watching . . . and so, for that matter, is God.

A holy life will produce the deepest impression. Lighthouses blow no horns; they only shine.

D. L. Moody

GOD AND FAMILY

Let the Word of Christ—the Message—have the run of the house. Give it plenty of room in your lives.

Colossians 3:16 MSG

These are difficult days for our nation and for our families. But, thankfully, God is bigger than all of our challenges. God loves us and protects us. In times of trouble, He comforts us; in times of sorrow, He dries our tears. When we are troubled or weak or sorrowful, God is as near as our next breath.

Are you concerned for the well-being of your family? You are not alone. We live in a world where temptation and danger seem to lurk on every street corner. Parents and children alike have good reason to be watchful. But, despite the evils of our time, God remains steadfast. Even in these difficult days, no problem is too big for God.

As the first community to which a person is attached and the first authority under which a person learns to live, the family established society's most basic values.

Charles Colson

THE LAST WORD

For God has not given us a spirit of fear and timidity, but of power, love, and self-discipline. So you must never be ashamed to tell others about our Lord.

2 Timothy 1:7-8 NLT

All of us may find our courage tested by the inevitable disappointments and tragedies of life. After all, ours is a world filled with uncertainty, hardship, sickness, and danger. Old Man Trouble, it seems, is never too far from the front door.

When we focus upon our fears and our doubts, we may find many reasons to lie awake at night and fret about the uncertainties of the coming day. A better strategy, of course, is to focus not upon our fears but, instead, upon our God.

God is your shield and your strength; you are His forever. So don't focus your thoughts upon the fears of the day. Instead, trust God's plan and His eternal love for you. And remember: God is good, and He has the last word.

Fear is a self-imposed prison that will keep you from becoming what God intends for you to be.

Rick Warren

THE WISDOM TO FORGIVE

Be even-tempered, content with second place, quick to forgive an offense. Forgive as quickly and completely as the Master forgave you.

Colossians 3:13 MSG

When people behave badly, it's hard to forgive them. How hard? Sometimes, it's very hard! But God tells us that we must forgive other people, even when we'd rather not. So, if you're angry with anybody (or if you're upset by something you yourself have done), it's now time to forgive.

God instructs you to treat other people exactly as you wish to be treated. And since you want to be forgiven for the mistakes that you make, you must be willing to extend forgiveness to other people for the mistakes that they have made. If you can't seem to forgive someone, you should keep asking God to help you until you do. And you can be sure of this: if you keep asking for God's help, He will give it.

Satan can't stop forgiveness from the throne to the sinner, but he can hinder forgiveness from one believer to another.

Franklin Graham

THE SHEPHERD'S CARE

For Your righteousness, O God, reaches to the heavens, You who have done great things.

Psalm 71:19 NASB

It's a promise that is made over and over again in the Bible: Whatever "it" is, God can handle it.

Life isn't always easy. Far from it! Sometimes, life can be very, very difficult. But even then, even during our darkest moments, we're protected by a loving Heavenly Father. When we're worried, God can reassure us; when we're sad, God can comfort us. When our hearts are broken, God is not just near; He is here. So we must lift our thoughts and prayers to Him. When we do, He will answer our prayers. Why? Because He is our Shepherd, and He has promised to protect us now and forever.

He is always thinking about us. We are before his eyes. The Lord's eye never sleeps, but is always watching out for our welfare. We are continually on his heart.

C. H. *Spurgeon*

BLESSED BEYOND MEASURE

The LORD *bless you and keep you; The* LORD *make His face shine upon you, And be gracious to you.*

Numbers 6:24-25 NKJV

Have you counted your blessings lately? You should. Of course, God's gifts are too numerous to count, but as a Christian, you should attempt to count them nonetheless. Your blessings include life, family, friends, talents, and possessions, for starters. And your greatest gift—a treasure that was paid for on the cross and is yours for the asking—is God's gift of salvation through Christ Jesus.

As believing Christians, we have all been blessed beyond measure. Thus, thanksgiving should become a habit, a regular part of our daily routines. Today, let us pause and thank our Creator for His blessings. And let us demonstrate our gratitude to the Giver of all things good by using His gifts for the glory of His kingdom.

God's love for His children in unconditional, no strings attached. But, God's blessings on our lives do come with a condition—obedience.

Jim Gallery

TRUST HIM TO GUIDE YOU

Trust the LORD *your God with all your heart and lean not on your own understanding; in all your ways acknowledge him, and he will make your paths straight.*

Proverbs 3:5-6 NIV

As Christians whose salvation has been purchased by the blood of Christ, we have every reason to live joyously and courageously. After all, Christ has already fought and won our battle for us—He did so on the cross at Calvary. But despite Christ's sacrifice, and despite God's promises, we may become confused or disoriented by the endless complications and countless distractions of life here in the 21st-century.

If you're unsure of your next step, lean upon God's promises and lift your prayers to Him. Remember that God is your protector. Open yourself to His heart, and trust Him to guide you. When you do, God will direct your steps, and you will receive His blessings today, tomorrow, and throughout eternity.

God will prove to you how good and acceptable and perfect His will is when He's got His hands on the steering wheel of your life.

Stuart & Jill Briscoe

ULTIMATE PROTECTION

God is striding ahead of you. He's right there with you. He won't let you down; he won't leave you. Don't be intimidated. Don't worry.

Deuteronomy 31:8 MSG

God has promised to protect us, and He intends to fulfill His promise. In a world filled with dangers and temptations, God is the ultimate armor. In a world filled with misleading messages, God's Word is the ultimate truth. In a world filled with more frustrations than we can count, God's Son offers the ultimate peace.

Will you accept God's peace and wear God's armor against the dangers of our world? Hopefully so, because when you do, you can live courageously, knowing that you possess the ultimate protection: God's unfailing love for you.

There is no safer place to live than the center of His will.

Calvin Miller

We are never out of reach of Satan's devices, so we must never be without the whole armor of God.

Warren Wiersbe

PERSPECTIVE IN PROBLEMS

It is important to look at things from God's point of view.

1 Corinthians 4:6 MSG

If a temporary loss of perspective has left you worried, exhausted, or both, it's time to readjust your thought patterns. Negative thoughts are habit-forming; thankfully, so are positive ones. With practice, you can form the habit of focusing on God's priorities and your possibilities. When you do, you'll soon discover that you will spend less time fretting about your challenges and more time praising God for His gifts.

When you call upon the Lord and prayerfully seek His will, He will give you wisdom and perspective. When you make God's priorities your priorities, He will direct your steps and calm your fears. So today and every day hereafter, pray for a sense of balance and perspective. And remember: no problems are too big for God—and that includes yours.

Earthly fears are no fears at all. Answer the big question of eternity, and the little questions of life fall into perspective.

Max Lucado

GOD WANTS TO USE YOU

To everything there is a season, a time for every purpose under heaven . . . .

Ecclesiastes 3:1 NKJV

God has things He wants you to do and places He wants you to go. The most important decision of your life is your commitment to accept Jesus Christ as your personal Lord and Savior. And, once your eternal destiny is secured, you will undoubtedly ask yourself the question "What's next?" If you earnestly seek God's will for your life, you will find it . . . in time.

You may be certain that God is planning to use you in surprising, wonderful ways. And you may be certain that He intends to lead you along a path of His choosing. Your task is to watch for His signs, to listen to His words, to obey His commandments, and to follow where He leads.

The place where God calls you is the place where your deep gladness and the world's deep hunger meet.

Frederick Buechner

THE POWER OF WORDS

The wise don't tell everything they know, but the foolish talk too much and are ruined.

Proverbs 10:14 NCV

All too often, in the rush to have ourselves heard, we speak first and think next . . . with unfortunate results. God's Word reminds us that, "Reckless words pierce like a sword, but the tongue of the wise brings healing" (Proverbs 12:18 NIV). If we seek to be a source of encouragement to friends and family, then we must measure our words carefully. Words are important: they can hurt or heal. Words can uplift us or discourage us, and reckless words, spoken in haste, cannot be erased.

Today, measure your words carefully. Use words of kindness and praise, not words of anger or derision. Remember that you have the power to heal others or to injure them, to lift others up or to hold them back. When you lift them up, your wisdom will bring healing and comfort to a world that needs both.

Christlikeness is not produced by imitation, but by inhabitation.

Rick Warren

DOERS OF THE WORD

But prove yourselves doers of the word, and not merely hearers.

James 1:22 NASB

The old saying is both familiar and true: actions speak louder than words. And as believers, we must beware: our actions should always give credence to the changes that Christ can make in the lives of those who walk with Him.

God calls upon each of us to act in accordance with His will and with respect for His commandments. If we are to be responsible believers, we must realize that it is never enough simply to hear the instructions of God; we must also live by them. And it is never enough to wait idly by while others to do God's work here on earth; we, too, must act. Doing God's work is a responsibility that each of us must bear, and when we do, our loving Heavenly Father rewards our efforts with a bountiful harvest.

Action springs not from thought, but from a readiness for responsibility.

Dietrich Bonhoeffer

CHOOSING THE GOOD LIFE

Most assuredly, I say to you, whatever you ask the Father in My name He will give you.

John 16:23 NKJV

God offers us abundance through His Son, Jesus. Whether or not we accept God's abundance is, of course, up to each of us. When we entrust our hearts and our days to the One who created us, we experience abundance through the grace and sacrifice of His Son, Jesus. But, when we turn our thoughts and our energies away from God's commandments, we inevitably forfeit the spiritual abundance that might otherwise be ours.

What is your focus today? Are you focused on God's Word and His will for your life? Or are you focused on the distractions and temptations of a difficult world. The answer to this question will, to a surprising extent, determine the quality and the direction of your day.

If you sincerely seek the spiritual abundance that your Savior offers, then follow Him completely and without reservation. When you do, you will receive the love, the life, and the abundance that He has promised.

SERENITY NOW

The Lord says, "Forget what happened before, and do not think about the past. Look at the new thing I am going to do. It is already happening. Don't you see it? I will make a road in the desert and rivers in the dry land."

Isaiah 43:18-19 NCV

As a spiritual being, you have the potential to grow in your personal knowledge of the Lord every day that you live. You can do so through prayer, through worship, through an openness to God's Holy Spirit, and through a careful study of God's Holy Word.

Your Bible contains powerful prescriptions for everyday living. If you sincerely seek to walk with God, you should commit yourself to the thoughtful study of His teachings. The Bible can and should be your roadmap for every aspect of your life.

Do you seek to establish a closer relationship with your Heavenly Father? Then study His Word every day, with no exceptions. The Holy Bible is a priceless, one-of-a-kind gift from God. Treat it that way and read it that way.

A PRICELESS TREASURE

Man shall not live by bread alone, but by every word that proceeds from the mouth of God.

Matthew 4:4 NKJV

The Bible is a priceless gift, a tool for Christians to use as they share the Good News of their Savior, Christ Jesus. Too many Christians, however, keep their spiritual tool kits tightly closed and out of sight.

Jonathan Edwards advised, "Be assiduous in reading the Holy Scriptures. This is the fountain whence all knowledge in divinity must be derived. Therefore let not this treasure lie by you neglected."

God's Holy Word is, indeed, a priceless, one-of-a-kind treasure. Handle it with care, but more importantly, handle it every day . . . starting today.

The promises of Scripture are not mere pious hopes or sanctified guesses. They are more than sentimental words to be printed on decorated cards for Sunday School children. They are eternal verities. They are true. There is no perhaps about them.

Peter Marshall

WHAT DOESN'T CHANGE

Jesus Christ is the same yesterday and today and forever.

Hebrews 13:8 NASB

Our world is in a state of constant change. God is not. At times, the world seems to be trembling beneath our feet. But we can be comforted in the knowledge that our Heavenly Father is the rock that cannot be shaken. His Word promises, "I am the LORD, I do not change" (Malachi 3:6 NKJV).

Every day that we live, we mortals encounter a multitude of changes—some good, some not so good, some downright disheartening. On those occasions when we must endure life-changing personal losses that leave us breathless, there is a place we can turn for comfort and assurance—we can turn to God. When we do, our loving Heavenly Father stands ready to protect us, to comfort us, to guide us, and, in time, to heal us.

In a world kept chaotic by change, you will eventually discover, as I have, that this is one of the most precious qualities of the God we are looking for: He doesn't change.

Bill Hybels

CHEERFULNESS 101

When a man is gloomy, everything seems to go wrong; when he is cheerful, everything seems right!

Proverbs 15:15 TLB

Few things in life are more sad or, for that matter, more absurd than a grumpy Christian. Christ promises us lives of abundance and joy, but He does not force His joy upon us. We must claim His joy for ourselves, and when we do, Jesus, in turn, fills our spirits with His power and His love.

How can we receive from Christ the joy that is rightfully ours? By giving Him what is rightfully His: our hearts and our souls.

When we earnestly commit ourselves to the Savior of mankind, when we place Jesus at the center of our lives and trust Him as our personal Savior, He will transform us, not just for today, but for all eternity. Then we, as God's children, can share Christ's joy and His message with a world that needs both.

Cheerfulness strengthens the heart and makes us try harder to have a good life, thus God's servants must always be in good spirits.

St. Philip Neri

A GROWING RELATIONSHIP WITH GOD

But grow in the grace and knowledge of our Lord and Savior Jesus Christ.

2 Peter 3:18 NIV

Your relationship with God is ongoing; it unfolds day by day, and it offers countless opportunities to grow closer to Him . . . or not. As each new day unfolds, you are confronted with a wide range of decisions: how you will behave, where you will direct your thoughts, with whom you will associate, and what you will choose to worship. These choices, along with many others like them, are yours and yours alone. How you choose determines how your relationship with God will unfold.

Are you continuing to grow in your love and knowledge of the Lord, or are you "satisfied" with the current state of your spiritual health? Hopefully, you're determined to make yourself a growing Christian. Your Savior deserves no less, and neither, by the way, do you.

Being childlike is commendable. Being childish is unacceptable.

Charles Swindoll

INFINITE LOVE

For I am convinced that neither death, nor life, nor angels, nor principalities, nor things present, nor things to come, nor powers, nor height, nor depth, nor any other created thing, will be able to separate us from the love of God, which is in Christ Jesus our Lord.

Romans 8:38-39 NASB

Christ's love for you is personal. He loves you so much that He gave His life in order that you might spend all eternity with Him. Christ loves you individually and intimately; His is a love unbounded by time or circumstance. Are you willing to experience an intimate relationship with Him? Your Savior is waiting patiently; don't make Him wait a single minute longer. Embrace His love today.

So Jesus came, stripping himself of everything as he came—omnipotence, omniscience, omnipresence—everything except love. "He emptied himself" (Philippians 2:7), emptied himself of everything except love. Love—his only protection, his only weapon, his only method.

E. Stanley Jones

NO COMPLAINTS

Do everything without complaining or arguing. Then you will be innocent and without any wrong.

Philippians 2:14-15 NCV

Because we are imperfect human beings, we often lose sight of our blessings. Ironically, most of us have more blessings than we can count, but we may still find reasons to complain about the minor frustrations of everyday life. To do so, of course, is not only wrong; it is also the pinnacle of shortsightedness and a serious roadblock on the path to spiritual abundance.

Are you tempted to complain about the inevitable minor frustrations of everyday living? Don't do it! Today and every day, make it a practice to count your blessings, not your hardships. It's the truly decent way to live.

Life is too short to nurse one's misery. Hurry across the lowlands so that you may spend more time on the mountaintops.

Phillips Brooks

Jesus wept, but he never complained.

C. H. Spurgeon

THE BATTLE HAS BEEN WON

Cast your burden upon the LORD and He will sustain you: He will never allow the righteous to be shaken.

Psalm 55:22 NASB

Christians have every reason to live courageously. After all, the ultimate battle has already been won on the cross at Calvary. But even dedicated followers of Christ may find their courage tested by the inevitable disappointments and fears that visit the lives of believers and non-believers alike.

When you find yourself worried about the challenges of today or the uncertainties of tomorrow, you must ask yourself whether or not you are ready to place your concerns and your life in God's all-powerful, all-knowing, all-loving hands. If the answer to that question is yes—as it should be—then you can draw courage today from the source of strength that never fails: your Heavenly Father.

Seeing that a Pilot steers the ship in which we sail, who will never allow us to perish even in the midst of shipwrecks, there is no reason why our minds should be overwhelmed with fear and overcome with weariness.

John Calvin

SOLVING THE RIDDLES

If you need wisdom—if you want to know what God wants you to do—ask him, and he will gladly tell you. He will not resent your asking.

James 1:5 NLT

Life presents each of us with countless questions, conundrums, doubts, and problems. Thankfully, the riddles of everyday living are not too difficult to solve if we look for answers in the right places. When we have questions, we should consult God's Word, we should seek the guidance of the Holy Spirit, and we should trust the counsel of God-fearing friends and family members.

Are you facing a difficult decision? Take your concerns to God and avail yourself of the messages and mentors that He has placed along your path. When you do, God will speak to you in His own way and in His own time, and when He does, you can most certainly trust the answers that He gives.

As we trust God to give us wisdom for today's decisions, He will lead us a step at a time into what He wants us to be doing in the future.

Theodore Epp

BE STILL

Be still, and know that I am God.

Psalm 46:10 NKJV

Do you take time each day for an extended period of silence? And during those precious moments, do you sincerely open your heart to your Creator? If so, you are wise and you are blessed.

The world can be a noisy place, a place filled to the brim with distractions, interruptions, and frustrations. And if you're not careful, the struggles and stresses of everyday living can rob you of the peace that should rightfully be yours because of your personal relationship with Christ. So take time each day to quietly commune with your Savior. When you do, those moments of silence will enable you to participate more fully in the only source of peace that endures: God's peace.

Most of man's trouble comes from his inability to be still.

Blaise Pascal

Be quiet enough to hear God's whisper.

Anonymous

YOUR WILL AND GOD'S WILL

People may make plans in their minds, but the Lord decides what they will do.

Proverbs 16:9 NCV

If you're like most people, you like being in control. You want things to happen according to your wishes and according to your timetable. But sometimes, God has other plans . . . and He always has the final word. Are you embittered by a personal tragedy that you did not deserve and cannot understand? If so, it's time to make peace with life. It's time to forgive others, and, if necessary, to forgive yourself. It's time to accept the unchangeable past, to embrace the priceless present, and to have faith in the promise of tomorrow. It's time to trust God completely. And it's time to reclaim the peace—His peace—that can and should be yours.

So if you've encountered unfortunate circumstances that are beyond your power to control, accept those circumstances . . . and trust God. When you do, you can be comforted in the knowledge that your Creator is both loving and wise, and that He understands His plans perfectly, even when you do not.

OUR ROCK IN TURBULENT TIMES

And he said: "The LORD is my rock and my fortress and my deliverer; the God of my strength, in whom I will trust . . . ."

2 Samuel 22:2-3 NKJV

Psalm 145 promises, "The Lord is near to all who call on him, to all who call on him in truth. He fulfills the desires of those who fear him; he hears their cry and saves them" (vv. 18-20 NIV). And the words of Jesus offer us comfort: "These things I have spoken to you, that in Me you may have peace. In the world you will have tribulation; but be of good cheer, I have overcome the world" (John 16:33 NKJV).

As believers, we know that God loves us and that He will protect us. In times of hardship, He will comfort us; in times of sorrow, He will dry our tears. When we are troubled or weak or sorrowful, God is always with us. We must build our lives on the rock that cannot be shaken: we must trust in God. And then, we must get on with the hard work of tackling our problems . . . because if we don't, who will? Or should?

The Rock of Ages is the great sheltering encirclement.

Oswald Chambers

ASK AND RECEIVE

Ask, and it will be given to you; seek, and you will find; knock, and it will be opened to you. For everyone who asks receives, and he who seeks finds, and to him who knocks it will be opened.

Matthew 7:7-8 NKJV

Are you a man who asks God for guidance and strength? If so, then you're continually inviting your Creator to reveal Himself in a variety of ways. As a follower of Christ, you must do no less.

Jesus made it clear to His disciples: they should petition God to meet their needs. So should we. Genuine, heartfelt prayer produces powerful changes in us and in our world. When we lift our hearts to God, we open ourselves to a never-ending source of divine wisdom and infinite love.

Do you have questions about your future that you simply can't answer? Do you have needs that you simply can't meet by yourself? Do you sincerely seek to know God's purpose for your life? If so, ask Him for direction, for protection, and for His strength. Whatever your need, no matter how great or small, pray about it and never lose hope. God is not just near; He is here, and He's perfectly capable of answering your prayers. Now, it's up to you to ask.

THE LIGHT UNTO YOUR PATH

All Scripture is inspired by God and profitable for teaching, for reproof, for correction, for training in righteousness; so that the man of God may be adequate, equipped for every good work.

2 Timothy 3:16-17 NASB

God has given us a guidebook for righteous living called the Holy Bible. It contains thorough instructions which, if followed, lead to fulfillment, righteousness, and salvation. But, if we choose to ignore God's commandments, the results are as predictable as they are tragic.

God has given us the Bible for the purpose of knowing His promises, His power, His commandments, His wisdom, His love, and His Son. As we study God's teachings and apply them to our lives, we live by the Word that shall never pass away.

Today, let us follow God's commandments, and let us conduct our lives in such a way that we might be shining examples to our families, and, to those who have not yet found Christ.

The Bible is the cradle wherein Christ is laid.

Martin Luther

PRIORITIES . . . MOMENT BY MOMENT

You can't go wrong when you love others. When you add up everything in the law code, the sum total is love. But make sure that you don't get so absorbed and exhausted in taking care of all your day-by-day obligations that you lose track of the time and doze off, oblivious to God.

Romans 13:10-11 MSG

God calls each of us to worship Him, to obey His commandments, and to accept His Son as our Savior. When we do so, God blesses us in ways that we can scarcely understand. But, when we allow the demands of the day to interfere with our communications with the Father, we unintentionally distance ourselves from our greatest source of abundance and peace.

If you've been too busy to spare even a few minutes with your Creator, it's officially time to rearrange your priorities by placing God first, not last. Every day provides opportunities to put God where He belongs: at the center of your thoughts and prayers. When you do so, you will worship your Creator, not just with words, but also with deeds. And then, just as He promised, God will bless you now and forever.

COURAGE DURING TIMES OF CHANGE

Therefore do not worry about tomorrow, for tomorrow will worry about itself. Each day has enough trouble of its own.

Matthew 6:34 NIV

All of us may face adversity, discouragement, or disappointment. And, through-out life, we must all endure life-changing personal losses that leave us breathless. When we do, God stands ready to protect us. Psalm 18:30 promises "As for God, His way is perfect; the word of the Lord is proven; He is a shield to all who trust in Him" (NKJV). When we are troubled, we must call upon God, and, in His own time and according to His own plan, He will heal us.

Times of adversity can also become times of intense personal and spiritual growth. In difficult times, we learn lessons that we could have learned in no other way: We learn about life, we learn about ourselves, and we learn about God's ability to renew our spirits and restore our strength.

Are you anxious? Take those anxieties to God. Are you troubled? Take your troubles to Him. The same God who created the universe will protect you if you ask Him . . . so ask Him.

SAYING YES TO THE FATHER

Fear thou not; for I am with thee.

Isaiah 41:10 KJV

Your decision to seek a deeper relationship with God will not remove all problems from your life; to the contrary, it will bring about a series of personal crises as you constantly seek to say "yes" to God although the world encourages you to do otherwise. Each time you are tempted to distance yourself from the Creator, you will face a spiritual crisis. A few of these crises may be monumental in scope, but most will be the small, everyday decisions of life. In fact, life here on earth can be seen as one test after another—and with each crisis comes yet another opportunity to grow closer to God . . . or to distance yourself from His plan for your life.

Today, you will face many opportunities to say "yes" to your Creator—and you will also encounter many opportunities to say "no" to Him. Your answers will determine the quality of your day and the direction of your life, so answer carefully . . . very carefully.

COMFORTING OTHERS

Carry each other's burdens, and in this way you will fulfill the law of Christ.

Galatians 6:2 NIV

The 118th Psalm reminds us, "This is the day which the Lord hath made; we will rejoice and be glad in it" (v. 24 KJV). As we rejoice in this day that the Lord has given us, let us remember that an important part of today's celebration is the time we spend comforting those in need.

Each day provides countless opportunities to encourage others and to assist those who need our help. When we do, we spread seeds of hope and happiness.

Today, when you encounter someone who needs a helping hand or a comforting word, be generous with both. You possess the power to make the world a better place one person—and one hug—at a time. When you use that power wisely, you make your own corner of the world a kinder, gentler, happier place.

A Christian is someone who shares the sufferings of God in the world.

Dietrich Bonhoeffer

THE INNER VOICE

Let us come near to God with a sincere heart and a sure faith, because we have been made free from a guilty conscience, and our bodies have been washed with pure water.

Hebrews 10:22 NCV

American humorist Josh Billings observed, "Reason often makes mistakes, but conscience never does." How true. Even when we deceive our neighbors, and even when we attempt to deceive ourselves, God has given each of us a conscience, a small, quiet voice that tells us right from wrong. We must listen to that inner voice . . . or else we must accept the consequences that inevitably befall those who choose to rebel against God.

He that loses his conscience has almost nothing left that is worth keeping.

Izaak Walton

The voice of the subconscious argues with you, tries to convince you; but the inner voice of God does not argue; it does not try to convince you. It just speaks, and it is self-authenticating.

E. Stanley Jones

COURTESY MATTERS

Out of respect for Christ, be courteously reverent to one another.

Ephesians 5:21 MSG

Did Christ instruct us in matters of etiquette and courtesy? Of course He did. Christ's instructions are clear: "In everything, therefore, treat people the same way you want them to treat you, for this is the Law and the Prophets" (Matthew 7:12 NASB). Jesus did not say, "In some things, treat people as you wish to be treated." And, He did not say, "From time to time, treat others with kindness." Christ said that we should treat others as we wish to be treated in every aspect of our daily lives. This, of course, is a tall order indeed, but as Christians, we are commanded to do our best.

Today, be a little kinder than necessary to family members, friends, and total strangers. And, as you consider all the things that Christ has done in your life, honor Him with your words and with your deeds. He expects no less, and He deserves no less.

Only the courteous can love, but it is love that makes them courteous.

C. S. Lewis

THE IMPORTANCE OF DISCIPLINE

Discipline yourself for the purpose of godliness.

1 Timothy 4:7 NASB

Are you a self-disciplined person? If so, congratulations . . . your disciplined approach to life can help you build a more meaningful relationship with God. Why? Because God expects all His believers (including you) to lead lives of disciplined obedience to Him . . . and He rewards those believers who do.

Sometimes, it's hard to be dignified and disciplined. Why? Because you live in a world where many prominent people want you to believe that dignified, self-disciplined behavior is going out of style. But don't deceive yourself: self-discipline never goes out of style.

Your greatest accomplishments will probably require plenty of work and a heaping helping of self-discipline—which, by the way, is perfectly fine with God. After all, He knows that you're up to the task, and He has big plans for you. God will do His part to fulfill those plans, and the rest, of course, depends upon you.

THE POWER OF FAITH

Have faith in the LORD your God and you will be upheld.

2 Chronicles 20:20 NIV

Every life—including yours—is a series of successes and failures, celebrations and disappointments, joys and sorrows. Every step of the way, through every triumph and tragedy, God will stand by your side and strengthen you . . . if you have faith in Him. Jesus taught His disciples that if they had faith, they could move mountains. You can too.

When you place your faith, your trust, indeed your life in the hands of Christ Jesus, you'll be amazed at the marvelous things He can do with you and through you. So strengthen your faith through praise, through worship, through Bible study, and through prayer. And trust God's plans. With Him, all things are possible, and He stands ready to open a world of possibilities to you . . . if you have faith.

Let your faith in Christ be in the quiet confidence that He will, every day and every moment, give you the strength you need.

Andrew Murray

GOD'S GIFT OF FAMILY

You must choose for yourselves today whom you will serve . . . as for me and my family, we will serve the Lord.

Joshua 24:15 NCV

In the life of every family, there are moments of frustration and disappointment. Lots of them. But, for those who are lucky enough to live in the presence of a close-knit, caring clan, the rewards far outweigh the frustrations.

No family is perfect, and neither is yours. But, despite the inevitable challenges and hurt feelings of family life, your clan is God's gift to you. That little band of men, women, kids, and babies is a priceless treasure on temporary loan from the Father above. Give thanks to the Giver for the gift of family . . . and act accordingly.

The only true source of meaning in life is found in love for God and his son Jesus Christ, and love for mankind, beginning with our own families.

James Dobson

Whole-life stewardship means putting the purposes of God at the very center of our lives and families.

Tom Sine

THE FINANCIAL GUIDE

The blessing of the L*ORD makes one rich . . . .*

Proverbs 10:22 NKJV

God's Word is not only a roadmap to eternal life; it is also an indispensable guidebook for life here on earth. As such, the Bible has much to say about your life and your finances.

God's Word can be a roadmap to a place of righteousness and abundance. Make it your roadmap. God's wisdom can be a light to guide your steps. Claim it as your light. God's Word can be an invaluable tool for crafting a better day and a better life. Make it your tool. And finally, God's Word can help you organize your financial life in such a way that you have less need to worry and more time to celebrate His glorious creation. If that sounds appealing, open your Bible, read its instructions, and follow them.

It is easy to determine the importance money plays in God's plan by the abundance of Scripture that relates to it—more than seven hundred verses directly refer to its use.

Larry Burkett

THE JOYS OF FRIENDSHIP

I thank my God every time I remember you.

Philippians 1:3 NIV

What is a friend? The dictionary defines the word *friend* as "a person who is attached to another by feelings of affection or personal regard." This definition is accurate, as far as it goes, but when we examine the deeper meaning of friendship, so many more descriptors come to mind: trustworthiness, loyalty, helpfulness, kindness, encouragement, humor, and cheerfulness, to mention but a few.

Today, as you consider the many blessings that God has given you, remember to thank Him for the friends He has chosen to place along your path. May you be a blessing to them, and may they richly bless you today, tomorrow, and every day that you live.

No medicine is more valuable, none more efficacious, none better suited to the cure of all our temporal ills than a friend to whom we may turn for consolation in time of trouble.

St. Aelred

HIS GENEROSITY . . . AND YOURS

But God demonstrates his own love for us in this: While we were still sinners, Christ died for us.

Romans 5:8 NIV

Jesus Christ showed His love for us by willingly sacrificing His own life so that we might have eternal life. We, as Christ's followers, are challenged to share His love. And, when we walk each day with Jesus—and obey the commandments found in God's Holy Word—we are worthy ambassadors for Him.

Just as Christ has been—and will always be—the ultimate friend to His flock, so should we be Christlike in our love and generosity to those in need. When we share the love of Christ, we share a priceless gift. As His servants, we must do no less.

If we have the true love of God in our hearts, we will show it in our lives. We will not have to go up and down the earth proclaiming it. We will show it in everything we say or do.

D. L. Moody

HIS CALLING

But as God has distributed to each one, as the Lord has called each one, so let him walk.

1 Corinthians 7:17 NKJV

It is terribly important that you heed God's calling by discovering and developing your talents and your spiritual gifts. If you seek to make a difference—and if you seek to bear eternal fruit—you must discover your gifts and begin using them for the glory of God.

Every believer has at least one gift. In John 15:16, Jesus says, "You did not choose Me, but I chose you and appointed you that you should go and bear fruit, and that your fruit should remain, that whatever you ask the Father in My name He may give you." Have you found your special calling? If not, keep searching and keep praying until you find it. God has important work for you to do, and the time to begin that work is now.

When you become consumed by God's call on your life, everything will take on new meaning and significance. You will begin to see every facet of your life, including your pain, as a means through which God can work to bring others to Himself.

Charles Stanley

GOD IS LOVE

He who does not love does not know God, for God is love.

1 John 4:8 NKJV

God loves you. He loves you more than you can imagine; His affection is deeper than you can fathom. God made you in His own image and gave you salvation through the person of His Son Jesus. And as a result, you have an important decision to make. You must decide what to do about God's love: you can return it . . . or not.

When you accept the love that flows from the heart of God, you are transformed. When you embrace God's love, you feel differently about yourself, your neighbors, your community, your church, and your world. When you open your heart to God's love, you will feel compelled to share God's message—and His compassion—with others. God's heart is overflowing—accept His love; return His love; and share His love.

If nothing in us can win Thy love, nothing in the universe can prevent Thee from loving us. Thy love is uncaused and undeserved. Thou art Thyself the reason for the love wherewith we are loved.

A. W. Tozer

STANDING ON THE ROCK

He heals the brokenhearted and bandages their wounds.

Psalm 147:3 NCV

God loves us and protects us. In times of trouble, He comforts us; in times of sorrow, He dries our tears. Psalm 147 promises, "He heals the brokenhearted, and binds their wounds" (v. 3, NASB). When we are troubled, we must call upon God, and—in His own time and according to His own plan—He will heal us.

Do you feel fearful or weak or sorrowful? Are you discouraged or bitter? Do you feel "stuck" in a place that is uncomfortable for you? If so, remember that God is as near as your next breath. So trust Him and turn to Him for solace, for security, and for salvation. And build your life on the rock that cannot be shaken . . . that rock is God.

If the Father knows when a sparrow falls, don't you think He's aware of where you are, what your need is, and what your concern is? Rest in that.

Jack Hayford

LET THE CELEBRATION BEGIN

I've told you these things for a purpose: that my joy might be your joy, and your joy wholly mature.

John 15:11 MSG

Oswald Chambers correctly observed, "Joy is the great note all throughout the Bible." C. S. Lewis echoed that thought when he wrote, "Joy is the serious business of heaven." But, even the most dedicated Christians can, on occasion, forget to celebrate each day for what it is: a priceless gift from God.

Today, let us be joyful Christians with smiles on our faces and kind words on our lips. After all, this is God's day, and He has given us clear instructions for its use. We are commanded to rejoice and be glad. So, with no further ado, let the celebration begin . . . .

Celebration is possible only through the deep realization that life and death are never found completely separate. Celebration can really come about only where fear and love, joy and sorrow, tear and smiles can exist together.

Henri Nouwen

THE GREATEST OF THESE

But now abide faith, hope, love, these three; but the greatest of these is love.

1 Corinthians 13:13 NASB

The familiar words of 1st Corinthians 13 remind us of the importance of love. Faith is important, of course. So too is hope. But love is more important still.

Christ showed His love for us on the cross, and, as Christians, we are called upon to return Christ's love by sharing it. We are commanded (not advised, not encouraged . . . commanded!) to love one another just as Christ loved us (John 13:34). That's a tall order, but as Christians, we are obligated to follow it.

Sometimes love is easy (puppies and sleeping children come to mind) and sometimes love is hard (fallible human beings come to mind). But God's Word is clear: We are to love our all our friends and neighbors, not just the lovable ones. So today, take time to spread Christ's message by word and by example. And the greatest of these is, of course, is example.

THE LESSONS OF TOUGH TIMES

I waited patiently for the LORD; he turned to me and heard my cry. He lifted me out of the slimy pit, out of the mud and mire; he set my feet on a rock and gave me a firm place to stand. He put a new song in my mouth, a hymn of praise to our God . . . .

Psalm 40:1-3 NIV

We are imperfect beings living in an imperfect world; mistakes are simply part of the price we pay for being here. Yet, even though mistakes are an inevitable part of life's journey, repeated mistakes should not be. When we commit the inevitable blunders of life, we must correct them, learn from them, and pray for the wisdom to avoid those same mistakes in the future. If we are successful, our missteps become lessons, and our lives become adventures in growth.

Mistakes are the price we pay for being human; repeated mistakes are the price we pay for being stubborn. But, if we are wise enough to learn from our experiences, we continue to mature throughout every stage of life. And that's precisely what God intends for us to do.

Father, take our mistakes and turn them into opportunities.

Max Lucado

I NEED PATIENCE . . . NOW!

We urge you, brethren, admonish the unruly, encourage the fainthearted, help the weak, be patient with everyone.

1 Thessalonians 5:14 NASB

Most of us are impatient for God to grant us the desires of our heart. Usually, we know what we want, and we know precisely when we want it: right now, if not sooner. But God may have other plans. And when God's plans differ from our own, we must trust in His infinite wisdom and in His infinite love.

As busy men living in a fast-paced world, many of us find that waiting quietly for God is difficult. But God instructs us to be patient in all things. We must be patient with our families, our friends, and our associates. We must also be patient with our Creator as He unfolds His plan for our lives. And that's as it should be. After all, think about how patient God has been with us.

Our challenge is to wait in faith for the day of God's favor and salvation.

Jim Cymbala

YOUR TRAVELING COMPANION

But thanks be to God, who gives us the victory through our Lord Jesus Christ. Therefore, my beloved brethren, be steadfast, immovable, always abounding in the work of the Lord, knowing that your labor is not in vain in the Lord.

1 Corinthians 15:57-58 NKJV

As you continue to seek God's purpose for your life, you will undoubtedly experience your fair share of disappointments, detours, false starts, and failures. When you do, don't become discouraged: God's not finished with you yet.

The old saying is as true today as it was when it was first spoken: "Life is a marathon, not a sprint." That's why wise travelers select a traveling companion who never tires and never falters. That partner, of course, is your Heavenly Father. So pray as if everything depended upon God, and work as if everything depended upon you. And trust God to do the rest.

By perseverance the snail reached the ark.

C. H. Spurgeon

LIFE ABUNDANT

I have come that they may have life, and that they may have it more abundantly.

John 10:10 NKJV

God offers us abundance, but He does not force it upon us. He promises that we "might have life" and that we "might have it more abundantly" if we accept His grace, His blessings, and His Son.

When we entrust our hearts and our days to the One who created us, we experience abundance through the grace and sacrifice of His Son Jesus. But, when we turn our thoughts and direct our energies away from God's commandments, we inevitably forfeit the spiritual abundance that might otherwise be ours.

Do you sincerely seek the riches that our Savior offers to those who give themselves to Him? Then follow Him completely and without reservation. When you do, you will receive the love and the abundance that He has promised.

Jesus wants Life for us, Life with a capital L.

John Eldredge

IN TIMES OF ADVERSITY

For whatever is born of God overcomes the world. And this is the victory that has overcome the world—our faith.

1 John 5:4 NKJV

All of us face times of adversity. On occasion, we all must endure the disappointments and tragedies that befall believers and nonbelievers alike. The reassuring words of 1 John 5:4 remind us that when we accept God's grace, we overcome the passing hardships of this world by relying upon His strength, His love, and His promise of eternal life.

When we face the inevitable difficulties of life here on earth, God stands ready to protect us. Our responsibility, of course, is to ask Him for protection. When we call upon Him in heartfelt prayer, He will answer—in His own time and according to His own plan—and He will heal us. And while we are waiting for God's plans to unfold and for His healing touch to restore us, we can be comforted in the knowledge that our Creator can overcome any obstacle, even if we cannot. Let us take God at His word, and let us trust Him.

ULTIMATE ACCOUNTABILITY

Walk in a manner worthy of the God who calls you into His own kingdom and glory.

1 Thessalonians 2:12 NASB

For most of us, it is a daunting thought: one day, perhaps soon, we'll come face-to-face with our Heavenly Father, and we'll be called to account for our actions here on earth. Our personal histories will certainly not be surprising to God; He already knows everything about us. But the full scope of our activities may be surprising to us: some of us will be pleasantly surprised; others will not be.

Today, do whatever you can to ensure that your thoughts and your deeds are pleasing to your Creator. Because you will, at some point in the future, be called to account for your actions. And the future may be sooner than you think.

Though I know intellectually how vulnerable I am to pride and power, I am the last one to know when I succumb to their seduction. That's why spiritual Lone Rangers are so dangerous—and why we must depend on trusted brothers and sisters who love us enough to tell us the truth.

Chuck Colson

NOURISHED BY THE WORD

You will be a good servant of Christ Jesus, constantly nourished on the words of the faith and of the sound doctrine which you have been following.

1 Timothy 4:6 NASB

As you look to the future and decide upon the direction of your life, what will you use as your roadmap? Will you trust God's Holy Word and use it as an indispensable tool to guide your steps? Or will you choose a different map to guide your steps? The map you choose will determine the quality of your journey and its ultimate destination.

The Bible is the ultimate guide for life; make it your guidebook as well. When you do, you can be comforted in the knowledge that your steps are guided by a Source of wisdom and truth that never fails.

God did not write a book and send it by messenger to be read at a distance by unaided minds. He spoke a Book and lives in His spoken words, constantly speaking His words and causing the power of them to persist across the years.

A. W. Tozer

TOO BUSY

Careful planning puts you ahead in the long run; hurry and scurry puts you further behind.

Proverbs 21:5 MSG

Are you making time each day to praise God and to study His Word? If so, you know firsthand the blessings that He offers those who worship Him consistently and sincerely. But, if you have unintentionally allowed the hustle and bustle of your busy day to come between you and your Creator, then you must slow down, take a deep breath, and rearrange your priorities.

God loved this world so much that He sent His Son to save it. And now only one real question remains for you: what will you do in response to God's love? The answer should be obvious: God must come first in your life. He is the giver of all good things, and He is the One who sent His Son so that you might have eternal life. He deserves your prayers, your obedience, your stewardship, and your love—and He deserves these things all day every day, not just on Sunday mornings.

We often become mentally and spiritually barren because we're so busy.

Franklin Graham

ALWAYS WITH US

For a child is born to us, a son is given to us. And the government will rest on his shoulders. These will be his royal titles: Wonderful Counselor, Mighty God, Everlasting Father, Prince of Peace.

Isaiah 9:6 NLT

Are you facing difficult circumstances or unwelcome changes? If so, please remember that God is far bigger than any problem you may face. So, instead of worrying about life's inevitable challenges, put your faith in the Father and His only begotten Son: "Jesus Christ is the same yesterday, today, and forever" (Hebrews 13:8 NKJV). And remember: it is precisely because your Savior does not change that you can face your challenges with courage for today and hope for tomorrow.

Life is often challenging, but as Christians, we should not be afraid. God loves us, and He will protect us. In times of hardship, He will comfort us; in times of change, He will guide our steps. When we are troubled or weak or sorrowful, God is always with us. We must build our lives on the rock that cannot be moved . . . we must trust in God. Always.

CHOICES, CHOICES, CHOICES

Cheerfully pleasing God is the main thing, and that's what we aim to do, regardless of our conditions.

2 Corinthians 5:9 MSG

Your life is a series of choices. From the instant you wake up in the morning until the moment you nod off to sleep at night, you make lots of decisions: decisions about the things you do, decisions about the words you speak, and decisions about the thoughts you choose to think. Simply put, the quality of those decisions determines the quality of your life.

So, if you sincerely want to lead a life that is pleasing to God, you must make choices that are pleasing to Him. He deserves no less . . . and neither, for that matter, do you.

I believe with all my heart and soul that at every important crossroads in my life I was faced with a choice: between right and wrong, between serving God and pleasing myself. I didn't always make the right choice. In fact, I stumbled down the wrong path more times than I marched down the right one. But God heard the earnest prayers of those who loved me and by His grace brought me to my knees.

Al Green

LOVE AND MARRIAGE

If you falter in times of trouble, how small is your strength!

Proverbs 24:10 NIV

In God's program, the words "love" and "commitment" are intertwined. According to God, genuine love is patient, unselfish, and kind, but it's goes beyond that—genuine love is committed love, and that means that genuine love is more than a feeling . . . it is a decision to make love endure, no matter what.

Unfortunately, we live in a world where marriage vows are taken far too lightly. Too many couples are far too quick to push the panic button—or the eject button.

If you're a married man who has vowed to love your partner "till death do you part," then you must take that vow very seriously. And one more thing: you'd better put God right where He belongs: at the absolute center of your marriage.

Commitment doesn't come easy, but when you're fighting for something you believe in, the struggle is worth it.

John Maxwell

TO LISTEN OR NOT LISTEN . . .

So I strive always to keep my conscience clear before God and man.

Acts 24:16 NIV

When you're about to do something that you know is wrong, a little voice inside your head has a way of speaking up. That voice, of course, is your conscience: an early-warning system designed to keep you out of trouble. If you listen to that voice, you'll be okay; if you ignore it, you're asking for headaches or heartbreaks, or both.

Whenever you're about to make an important decision, you should listen carefully to the quiet voice inside. Sometimes, of course, it's tempting to do otherwise. From time to time you'll be tempted to abandon your better judgement by ignoring your conscience. But remember: a conscience is a terrible thing to waste. So instead of ignoring that quiet little voice, pay careful attention to it. If you do, your conscience will lead you in the right direction—in fact, it's trying to lead you right now. So listen . . . and learn.

A quiet conscience sleeps in thunder.

Thomas Fuller

A FRESH OPPORTUNITY

When we were baptized, we were buried with Christ and shared his death. So, just as Christ was raised from the dead by the wonderful power of the Father, we also can live a new life.

Romans 6:4 NCV

God's Word is clear: When we genuinely invite Him to reign over our hearts, and when we accept His transforming love, we are forever changed. When we welcome Christ into our hearts, an old life ends and a new way of living—along with a completely new way of viewing the world—begins.

Each morning offers a fresh opportunity to invite Christ, yet once again, to rule over our hearts and our days. Each morning presents yet another opportunity to take up His cross and follow in His footsteps. Today, let us rejoice in the new life that is ours through Christ, and let us follow Him, step by step, on the path that He first walked.

When I met Christ, I felt that I had swallowed sunshine.

E. Stanley Jones

LET GOD DECIDE

A man's heart plans his way, but the LORD directs his steps.

Proverbs 16:9 NKJV

Are you facing a difficult decision, a troubling circumstance, or a powerful temptation? If so, it's time to step back, to stop focusing on the world, and to focus, instead, on the will of your Father in heaven. The world will often lead you astray, but God will not. His counsel leads you to Himself, which, of course, is the path He has always intended for you to take.

Everyday living is an exercise in decision-making. Today and every day you must make choices: choices about what you will do, what you will worship, and how you will think. When in doubt, make choices that you sincerely believe will bring you to a closer relationship with God. And if you're uncertain of your next step, pray about it. When you do, answers will come—the right answers for you.

The location of your affections will drive the direction of your decisions.

Lisa Bevere

THE POWER OF DILIGENCE

Do not lack diligence; be fervent in spirit; serve the Lord.

Romans 12:11 HCSB

God's Word reminds us again and again that our Creator expects us to lead disciplined lives. God doesn't reward laziness, misbehavior, or apathy. To the contrary, He expects believers to behave with dignity and discipline.

We live in a world in which leisure is glorified and indifference is often glamorized. But God has other plans. He did not create us for lives of mediocrity; He created us for far greater things.

Life's greatest rewards seldom fall into our laps; to the contrary, our greatest accomplishments usually require lots of work, which is perfectly fine with God. After all, He knows that we're up to the task, and He has big plans for us; may we, as disciplined believers, always be worthy of those plans.

No horse gets anywhere until he is harnessed. No life ever grows great until it is focused, dedicated, disciplined.

Harry Emerson Fosdick

AN INTENSELY BRIGHT FUTURE: YOURS

I came so they can have real and eternal life, more and better life than they ever dreamed of.

John 10:10 MSG

Are you excited about the opportunities of today and thrilled by the possibilities of tomorrow? Do you confidently expect God to lead you to a place of abundance, peace, and joy? And, when your days on earth are over, do you expect to receive the priceless gift of eternal life? If you trust God's promises, and if you have welcomed God's Son into your heart, then you believe that your future is intensely and eternally bright.

It takes courage to dream big dreams. You will discover that courage when you do three things: accept the past, trust God to handle the future, and make the most of the time He has given you today. No dreams are too big for God—not even yours. So start living—and dreaming—accordingly.

You cannot out-dream God.

John Eldredge

LIFE ETERNAL

Because I live, you will live also.

John 14:19 NASB

Eternal life is not an event that begins when you die. Eternal life begins when you invite Jesus into your heart right here on earth. So it's important to remember that God's plans for you are not limited to the ups and downs of everyday life. If you've allowed Jesus to reign over your heart, you've already begun your eternal journey.

As mere mortals, our vision for the future, like our lives here on earth, is limited. God's vision is not burdened by such limitations: His plans extend throughout all eternity.

Let us praise the Creator for His priceless gift, and let us share the Good News with all who cross our paths. We return our Father's love by accepting His grace and by sharing His message and His love. When we do, we are blessed here on earth and throughout all eternity.

Those of us who know the wonderful grace of redemption look forward to an eternity with God, when all things will be made new, when all our longings will at last find ultimate and final satisfaction.

Joseph Stowell

EXCELLENCE, NOT EXCUSES

Do you see a man skilled in his work? He will stand in the presence of kings.

Proverbs 22:29 HCSB

Excuses are everywhere . . . excellence is not. Your work is a picture book of your priorities. So whatever your job description, it's up to you, and no one else, to become masterful at your craft. It's up to you to do your job right, and to do it right now.

Because we humans are such creative excuse-makers, all of the best excuses have already been taken—we've heard them all before.

So if you're wasting your time trying to concoct a new and improved excuse, don't bother. It's impossible. A far better strategy is this: do the work. Now. Then, let your excellent work speak loudly and convincingly for itself.

Few things fire up a person's commitment like dedication to excellence.

John Maxwell

An excuse is only the skin of a reason stuffed with a lie.

Vance Havner

YOUR FAMILY NEEDS YOU

But if anyone does not provide for his own, and especially for those of his household, he has denied the faith and is worse than an unbeliever.

1 Timothy 5:8 NASB

The words of 1 Timothy 5:8 are unambiguous: if God has blessed us with families, then He expects us to care for them. Sometimes, this profound responsibility seems daunting. And sometimes, even for the most dedicated Christian men, family life holds moments of frustration and disappointment. But, for those who are lucky enough to live in the presence of a close-knit, caring clan, the rewards far outweigh the demands.

No family is perfect, and neither is yours. Despite the inevitable challenges of providing for your family, and despite the occasional hurt feelings of family life, your clan is God's gift to you. Give thanks to the Giver for the gift of family . . . and act accordingly.

God expresses His love by putting us in a family.

Charles Stanley

FIT TO SERVE

Whatever you eat or drink or whatever you do, you must do all for the glory of God.

1 Corinthians 10:31 NLT

We live in a world in which leisure is glorified and consumption is commercialized. But God has other plans. He did not create us for lives of gluttony or laziness; He created us for far greater things.

God has a plan for every aspect of your life, and His plan includes provisions for your physical health. But, He expects you to do your fair share of the work! In a world that is chock-full of tasty temptations, you may find it all too easy to make unhealthy choices. Your challenge, of course, is to resist those unhealthy temptations by every means you can, including prayer. And rest assured: when you ask for God's help, He will give it.

We have a world to explore and master, and we can't do it if our bodies are accumulating fat and our muscles, joints, and internal organs are breaking down. We need exercise.

Dr. Jordan S. Rubin

FORGIVE: IT'S GOD'S WAY

Be kind to one another, tender-hearted, forgiving each other, just as God in Christ also has forgiven you.

Ephesians 4:32 NASB

To forgive others is difficult. Being frail, fallible, imperfect human beings, we are quick to anger, quick to blame, slow to forgive, and even slower to forget. No matter. Forgiveness, no matter how difficult, is God's way, and it must be our way, too.

God's commandments are not intended to be customized for the particular whims of particular believers. God's Word is not a menu from which each of us may select items à la carte, according to our own desires. Far from it. God's Holy Word is a book that must be taken in its entirety; all of God's commandments are to be taken seriously. And, so it is with forgiveness. So, if you hold bitterness against even a single person, forgive. Then, to the best of your abilities, forget. It's God's way for you to live.

Looking back over my life, all I can see is mercy and grace written in large letters everywhere. May God help me have the same kind of heart toward those who wound or offend me.

Jim Cymbala

UNDENIABLE RICHES

God loves a cheerful giver.

2 Corinthians 9:7 NIV

God's Word commands us to be generous, compassionate servants to those who need our support. As believers, we have been richly blessed by our Creator. We, in turn, are called to share our gifts, our possessions, our testimonies, and our talents.

The theme of generosity is one of the cornerstones of Christ's teachings. If we are to be disciples of Christ, we, too, must be cheerful, generous, courageous givers. Our Savior expects no less from us. And He deserves no less.

The rich man is not one who possesses much, but one who gives much.

St. John Chrysostom

Think of the blessings we so easily take for granted: Life itself; preservation from danger; every bit of health we enjoy; every hour of liberty; the ability to see, to hear, to speak, to think, and to imagine all this comes from the hand of God.

Billy Graham

THE ULTIMATE GIFT

For it is by grace you have been saved, through faith—and this not from yourselves, it is the gift of God—not by works, so that no one can boast.

Ephesians 2:8-9 NIV

God has given us so many gifts, but none can compare with the gift of salvation. We have not earned our salvation; it is a gift from God. When we accept Christ into our hearts, we are saved by His grace.

God's grace is the ultimate gift, and we owe to Him the ultimate in thanksgiving. Let us praise the Creator for His priceless gift, and let us share the Good News with all who cross our paths. We return our Father's love by accepting His grace and by sharing His message and His love. When we do, we are eternally blessed . . . and the Father smiles.

The grace of God is sufficient for all our needs, for every problem, and for every difficulty, for every broken heart, and for every human sorrow.

Peter Marshall

SENSING HIS PRESENCE

Where can I go from your Spirit? Where can I flee from your presence? If I go up to the heavens, you are there; if I make my bed in the depths, you are there. If I rise on the wings of the dawn, if I settle on the far side of the sea, even there your hand will guide me, your right hand will hold me fast.

Psalm 139:7-10 NIV

If God is everywhere, why does He sometimes seem so far away? The answer to that question, of course, has nothing to do with God and everything to do with us.

When we begin each day on our knees, in praise and worship to Him, God often seems very near indeed. But, if we ignore God's presence or—worse yet—rebel against it altogether, the world in which we live becomes a spiritual wasteland.

Today, and every day hereafter, thank God and praise Him. He is the Giver of all things good. Wherever you are, whether you are happy or sad, victorious or vanquished, celebrate God's presence. And be comforted. For He is here.

God is nearer to me than I am to myself; my existence depends on the nearness and the presence of God.

Meister Eckhart

THE REMEDY FOR UNCERTAINTY

He replied, "You of little faith, why are you so afraid?" Then he got up and rebuked the winds and the waves, and it was completely calm.

Matthew 8:26 NIV

Sometimes, like Jesus' disciples, we feel threatened by the storms of life. During these moments, when we our hearts are flooded with uncertainty, we must remember that God is not simply near; He is here.

Have you ever felt your faith in God slipping away? If so, you are in good company. Even the most faithful Christians are, at times, beset by occasional bouts of discouragement and doubt. But even when you feel far removed from God, God never leaves your side. He is always with you, always willing to calm the storms of life. When you sincerely seek His presence—and when you genuinely seek to establish a deeper, more meaningful relationship with His Son—God will calm your fears, answer your prayers, and restore your soul.

Struggling with God over the issues of life doesn't' show a lack of faith—that is faith.

Lee Strobel

SHARING WORDS OF HOPE

Let's see how inventive we can be in encouraging love and helping out, not avoiding worshipping together as some do but spurring each other on.

Hebrews 10:24-25 MSG

Hope, like other human emotions, is contagious. When we associate with hope-filled Christians, we are encouraged by their faith and optimism. But, if we spend too much time in the company of naysayers and pessimists, our attitudes, like theirs, tend to be cynical and negative.

Are you a hopeful, optimistic, encouraging believer? And do you associate with like-minded people? Hopefully so. As a faithful follower of the One from Galilee, you have every reason to be hopeful, and you have every reason to share your hopes with others. So today, look for reasons to celebrate God's endless blessings. And while you're at it, look for people who will join you in the celebration. You'll be better for their company, and they'll be better for yours.

To the loved, a word of affection is a morsel, but to the love-starved, a word of affection can be a feast.

Max Lucado

THANKSGIVING YES . . . ENVY NO!

Stop your anger! Turn from your rage! Do not envy others—it only leads to harm.

Psalm 37:8 NLT

As the recipient of God's grace, you have every reason to celebrate life. After all, God has promised you the opportunity to receive His abundance and His joy—in fact, you have the opportunity to receive those gifts right now. But if you allow envy to gnaw away at the fabric of your soul, you'll find that joy remains elusive. So do yourself an enormous favor: Rather than succumbing to the sin of envy, focus on the marvelous things that God has done for you—starting with Christ's sacrifice. Thank the Giver of all good gifts, and keep thanking Him for the wonders of His love and the miracles of His creation. Count your own blessings and let your neighbors counts theirs. It's the godly way to live.

Contentment comes when we develop an attitude of gratitude for the important things we do have in our lives that we tend to take for granted if we have our eyes staring longingly at our neighbor's stuff.

Dave Ramsey

FAITH THAT MOVES MOUNTAINS

I tell you the truth, you can say to this mountain, "Go, fall into the sea." And if you have no doubts in your mind and believe that what you say will happen, God will do it for you.

Mark 11:23 NCV

Because we live in a demanding world, all of us have mountains to climb and mountains to move. Moving those mountains requires faith.

Are you a mountain mover whose faith is evident for all to see? Hopefully so. God needs more men who are willing to move mountains for His glory and for His kingdom.

God walks with you, ready and willing to strengthen you. Accept His strength today. And remember—Jesus taught His disciples that if they had faith, they could move mountains. You can too . . . so with no further ado, let the mountain-moving begin.

Only God can move mountains, but faith and prayer can move God.

E. M. Bounds

Faith is greater than learning.

Martin Luther

GIVING YOUR MARRIAGE AND FAMILY THE PLACE THEY DESERVE

Nevertheless, let every one of you in particular so love his wife even as himself; and the wife see that she reverence her husband.

Ephesians 5:33 KJV

It takes time to build a strong marriage . . . lots of time. Yet we live in a world where time seems to be an ever-shrinking commodity as we rush from place to place with seldom a moment to spare.

Has the busy pace of life robbed you of sufficient time with your loved ones? If so, it's time to adjust your priorities. And God can help.

When you allow God to help you organize your day, you'll soon discover that there is ample time for your spouse and your family. So, as you plan for the day ahead, make God's priorities your priorities. When you do, every other priority will have a tendency to fall neatly into place.

As you are married through the years, you can keep on falling in love—over and over again.

Ed Young

NEW BEGINNINGS

I will give you a new heart and put a new spirit in you . . . .

Ezekiel 36:26 NIV

If we sincerely want to change ourselves for the better, we must start on the inside and work our way out from there. Lasting change doesn't occur "out there"; it occurs "in here." It occurs, not in the shifting sands of our own particular circumstances, but in the quiet depths of our own hearts.

Are you in search of a new beginning or, for that matter, a new you? If so, don't expect changing circumstances to miraculously transform you into the person you want to become. Transformation starts with God, and it starts in the silent center of a humble human heart—like yours.

When we focus on God, the scene changes. He's in control of our lives; nothing lies outside the realm of His redemptive grace. Even when we make mistakes, fail in relationships, or deliberately make bad choices, God can redeem us.

Penelope J. Stokes

A LIGHT TO MY PATH

Your word is a lamp to my feet and a light to my path.

Psalm 119:105 NKJV

Are you a man who trusts God's Word without reservation? Hopefully so, because the Bible is unlike any other book—it is a guidebook for life here on earth and for life eternal. The Psalmist describes God's Word as, "a light to my path." Is the Bible your lamp? If not, you are depriving yourself of a priceless gift from the Creator.

Vance Havner observed, "It takes calm, thoughtful, prayerful meditation on the Word to extract its deepest nourishment." How true. God's Word can be a roadmap to a place of righteousness and abundance. Make it your roadmap. God's wisdom can be a light to guide your steps. Claim it as your light today, tomorrow, and every day of your life—and then walk confidently in the footsteps of God's only begotten Son.

Our nighttime passage through the dark and dangerous journey of this life is illuminated by God's Word, the Bible: "Your word is a lamp to my feet and light for my path" (Psalm 119:105). It is a light for our darkness and for our brighter times as well.

James Montgomery Boice

HAPPINESS AND HOLINESS

Happy are the people who live at your Temple . . . .
Happy are those whose strength comes from you.

Psalm 84:4-5 NKJV

Do you seek happiness, abundance, and contentment? If so, here are some things you should do: Love God and His Son; depend upon God for strength; try, to the best of your abilities, to follow God's will; and strive to obey His Holy Word. When you do these things, you'll discover that happiness goes hand-in-hand with righteousness. The happiest people are not those who rebel against God; the happiest people are those who love God and obey His commandments.

What does life have in store for you? A world full of possibilities (of course it's up to you to seize them), and God's promise of abundance (of course it's up to you to accept it). Your Creator has blessed you beyond measure. Honor Him with your prayers, your words, your deeds, and your joy.

To be in a state of true grace is to be miserable no more; it is to be happy forever. A soul in this state is a soul near and dear to God. It is a soul housed in God.

Thomas Brooks

THE WISDOM TO BE HUMBLE

Don't be selfish . . . . Be humble, thinking of others as better than yourself.

Philippians 2:3 NLT

God's Word clearly instructs us to be humble. And that's good because, as fallible human beings, we have so very much to be humble about! Yet some of us continue to puff ourselves up, seeming to say, "Look at me!" To do so is wrong.

As Christians, we have been refashioned and saved by Jesus Christ, and that salvation came not because of our own good works but because of God's grace. How, then, can we be prideful? The answer, of course, is that, if we are honest with ourselves and with our God, we simply can't be boastful . . . we must, instead, be eternally grateful and exceedingly humble. The good things in our lives, including our loved ones, come from God. He deserves the credit—and we deserve the glorious experience of giving it to Him.

It is very easy to overestimate the importance of our own achievements in comparison with what we owe others.

Dietrich Bonhoeffer

THE ATTITUDE OF A LEADER

Those who are wise will shine like the brightness of the heavens, and those who lead many to righteousness, like the stars for ever and ever.

Daniel 12:3 NIV

John Maxwell writes, "Great leaders understand that the right attitude will set the right atmosphere, which enables the right response from others." If you are in a position of leadership, whether as a father—or as a leader at your work, your church, or your school—it's up to you to set the right tone by maintaining the right attitude.

Our world needs Christian leaders, and so do your family members and co-workers. You can become a trusted, competent, thoughtful leader if you learn to maintain the right attitude: one that is realistic, optimistic, forward looking, and Christ-centered.

When God wants to accomplish something, He calls dedicated men and women to challenge His people and lead the way.

Warren Wiersbe

ON A MISSION FOR GOD

You are a chosen people. You are a kingdom of priests, God's holy nation, his very own possession. This is so you can show others the goodness of God, for he called you out of the darkness into his wonderful light.

1 Peter 2:9 NLT

Whether you realize it or not, you are on a personal mission for God. As a Christian, that mission is straightforward: Honor God, accept Christ as your personal Savior, and serve God's children.

Of course, you will encounter impediments as you attempt to discover the exact nature of God's purpose for your life, but you must never lose sight of the overriding purposes that God has established for all believers. You will encounter these overriding purposes again and again as you worship your Creator and study His Word.

Every day offers countless opportunities to serve God and to worship Him. When you do so, He will bless you in miraculous ways. May you continue to seek God's will, may you trust His word, and may you place Him where He belongs: at the very center of your life.

GLORIOUS OPPORTUNITIES

Make the most of every opportunity.

Colossians 4:5 NIV

Are you excited about the opportunities of today and thrilled by the possibilities of tomorrow? Do you confidently expect God to lead you to a place of abundance, peace, and joy? And, when your days on earth are over, do you expect to receive the priceless gift of eternal life? If you trust God's promises, and if you have welcomed God's Son into your heart, then you believe that your future is intensely and eternally bright.

Today, as you prepare to meet the duties of everyday life, pause and consider God's promises. And then think for a moment about the wonderful future that awaits all believers, including you. God has promised that your future is secure. Trust that promise, and celebrate the life of abundance and eternal joy that is now yours through Christ.

A wise man makes more opportunities than he finds.

Francis Bacon

TO GOD BE THE GLORY

God is against the proud, but he gives grace to the humble.

1 Peter 5:5 NCV

As Christians, we have a profound reason to be humble: We have been refashioned and saved by Jesus Christ, and that salvation came not because of our own good works but because of God's grace. Thus, we are not "self-made;" we are "God-made," and "Christ-saved." How, then, can we be boastful?

Dietrich Bonhoeffer observed, "It is very easy to overestimate the importance of our own achievements in comparison with what we owe others." In other words, reality breeds humility. So, instead of puffing out your chest and saying, "Look at me!" give credit where credit is due, starting with God. And, rest assured: There is no such thing as a self-made man. All of us are made by God . . . and He deserves the glory, not us.

A humble heart is like a magnet that draws the favor of God toward us.

Jim Cymbala

A DOSE OF LAUGHTER

A happy heart is like good medicine.

Proverbs 17:22 NCV

Laughter is God's gift, and He intends that we enjoy it. Yet sometimes, because of the inevitable stresses of everyday life, laughter seems only a distant memory. As Christians we have every reason to be cheerful and to be thankful. Our blessings from God are beyond measure, starting, of course, with a gift that is ours for the asking, God's gift of salvation through Christ Jesus.

Few things in life are more absurd than the sight of a grumpy Christian. So today, as you go about your daily activities, approach life with a smile and a chuckle. After all, God created laughter for a reason . . . and Father indeed knows best. So laugh!

Mirth is God's medicine. Everybody ought to bathe in it.

Henry Ward Beecher

When you have good, healthy relationships with your family and friends you're more prompted to laugh and not to take yourself so seriously.

Dennis Swanberg

THE CHAINS OF PERFECTIONISM

Those who wait for perfect weather will never plant seeds; those who look at every cloud will never harvest crops.

Ecclesiastes 11:4 NCV

The media delivers an endless stream of messages that tell you how to look, how to behave, and how to dress. The media's expectations are impossible to meet—God's are not. God doesn't expect perfection . . . and neither should you.

If you find yourself bound up by the chains of perfectionism, it's time to ask yourself who you're trying to impress, and why. If you're trying to impress other people, it's time to reconsider your priorities. Your first responsibility is to the Heavenly Father who created you and to His Son who saved you. Then, you bear a powerful responsibility to your family. But, when it comes to meeting society's unrealistic expectations, forget it! After all, pleasing God is simply a matter of obeying His commandments and accepting His Son. But as for pleasing everybody else? That's impossible!

FIRST THINGS FIRST

The thing you should want most is God's kingdom and doing what God wants. Then all these other things you need will be given to you.

Matthew 6:33 NCV

Have you fervently asked God to help prioritize your life? Have you asked Him for guidance and for the courage to do the things that you know need to be done? If so, then you're continually inviting your Creator to reveal Himself in a variety of ways. As a follower of Christ, you must do no less.

When you make God a full partner in every aspect of your life, He will lead you along the proper path: His path. When you allow God to reign over your heart, He will honor you with spiritual blessings that are simply too numerous to count. So, as you plan for the day ahead, make God's will your ultimate priority. When you do, your daily to-do list will take care of itself.

Our leisure, even our play, is a matter of serious concern. There is no neutral ground in the universe: every square inch, every split second, is claimed by God and counterclaimed by Satan.

C. S. Lewis

THE GREATEST AMONG US

So prepare your minds for service and have self-control.

1 Peter 1:13 NCV

Jesus teaches that the most esteemed men and women are not the leaders of society or the captains of industry. To the contrary, Jesus teaches that the greatest among us are those who choose to minister and to serve.

Today, you may feel the temptation to build yourself up in the eyes of your neighbors. Resist that temptation. Instead, serve your neighbors quietly and without fanfare. Then, when you have done your best to serve your community and to serve your God, you can rest comfortably knowing that in the eyes of God you have achieved greatness. And God's eyes, after all, are the only ones that really count.

Service is the pathway to real significance.

Rick Warren

If the attitude of servanthood is learned, by attending to God as Lord. Then, serving others will develop as a very natural way of life.

Eugene Peterson

THY WILL BE DONE

Shall I not drink from the cup the Father has given me?

John 18:11 NLT

When you encounter unfortunate circumstances that are beyond your power to control, here's a proven way to retain your sanity: accept those circumstances (no matter how unpleasant), and trust God.

The Theologian Reinhold Niebuhr composed a profoundly simple verse that came to be known as the Serenity Prayer: "God, grant me the serenity to accept the things I cannot change, the courage to change the things I can, and the wisdom to know the difference." Niebuhr's words are far easier to recite than they are to live by. Why? Because most of us want life to unfold in accordance with to our own wishes and timetables. But sometimes God has other plans.

When you trust God, you can be comforted in the knowledge that your Creator is both loving and wise, and that He understands His plans perfectly, even when you do not.

Our Lord never asks us to decide for Him; He asks us to yield to Him—a very different matter.

Oswald Chambers

WHERE IS GOD LEADING?

Dear brothers and sisters, whenever trouble comes your way, let it be an opportunity for joy. For when your faith is tested, your endurance has a chance to grow. So let it grow, for when your endurance is fully developed, you will be strong in character and ready for anything.

James 1:2-4 NLT

Whether we realize it or not, times of adversity can be times of intense personal and spiritual growth. Our difficult days are also times when we can learn and relearn some of life's most important lessons.

The next time you experience a difficult moment, a difficult day, or a difficult year, ask yourself this question: Where is God leading me? In times of struggle and sorrow, you can be certain that God is leading you to a place of His choosing. Your duty is to watch, to pray, to listen, and to follow.

A tried Christian grows rich by his losses, he rises by his falls, he lives by dying, and he becomes full by being emptied.

C. H. *Spurgeon*

BEYOND ANXIETY

In the multitude of my anxieties within me, Your comforts delight my soul.

Psalm 94:19 NKJV

God calls us to live above and beyond anxiety. God calls us to live by faith, not by fear. He instructs us to trust Him completely, this day and forever. But sometimes, trusting God is difficult, especially when we become caught up in the incessant demands of an anxious world.

When you feel anxious—and you will—return your thoughts to God's love. Then, take your concerns to Him in prayer, and to the best of your ability, leave them there. Whatever "it" is, God is big enough to handle it. Let Him. Now.

Worry and anxiety are sand in the machinery of life; faith is the oil.

E. Stanley Jones

Anxiety or excessive care for this world is a form of sin in the believer.

Harold Lindsell

WHY BAD THINGS?

They won't be afraid of bad news; their hearts are steady because they trust the Lord.

Psalm 112:7 NCV

If God is good, and if He made the world, why do bad things happen? Part of that question is easy to answer, and part of it isn't. Let's get to the easy part first: Sometimes, bad things happen because people disobey God's commandments and invite sadness and heartache into God's beautiful world.

But on other occasions, bad things happen, and it's nobody's fault. So who is to blame? Sometimes, nobody is to blame. Sometimes, things just happen and we simply cannot know why. Thankfully, all our questions will be answered . . . some day. The Bible promises that in heaven we will understand all the reasons behind God's plans. But until then, we must simply trust that God is good, and that, in the end, He will make things right.

There is but one good; that is God. Everything else is good when it looks to Him and bad when it turns from Him.

C. S. Lewis

FREEDOM FROM BITTERNESS

Don't insist on getting even; that's not for you to do. "I'll do the judging," says God. "I'll take care of it."

Romans 12:19 MSG

Bitterness is a spiritual sickness. It will consume your soul; it is dangerous to your emotional health. It can destroy you if you let it . . . so don't let it!

If you are caught up in intense feelings of anger or resentment, you know all too well the destructive power of these emotions. How can you rid yourself of these feelings? First, you must prayerfully ask God to cleanse your heart. Then, you must learn to catch yourself whenever thoughts of bitterness or hatred begin to attack you. Your challenge is this: You must learn to resist negative thoughts before they hijack your emotions.

Matthew 5:22 teaches us that if we judge our brothers and sisters, we, too, will be subject to judgement. Let us refrain, then, from judging our neighbors. Instead, let us forgive them and love them, while leaving their judgement to a far more capable authority: the One who sits on His throne in heaven.

UNBENDING TRUTH

So put away all falsehood and "tell your neighbor the truth" because we belong to each other.

Ephesians 4:25 NLT

We live in a world that presents us with countless temptations to wander far from God's path. These temptations have the potential to destroy us, in part, because they cause us to be dishonest with ourselves and with others.

Dishonesty is a habit. Once we start bending the truth, we're likely to keep bending it. A far better strategy, of course, is to acquire the habit of being completely forthright with God, with other people, and with ourselves.

Honesty is also a habit, a habit that pays powerful dividends for those who place character above convenience. So, the next time you're tempted to bend the truth—or to break it—ask yourself this simple question: "What does God want me to do?" Then listen carefully to your conscience. When you do, your actions will be honorable, and your character will take care of itself.

Never support an experience which does not have God as its source, and faith in God as its result.

Oswald Chambers

A SERIES OF CHOICES

The thing you should want most is God's kingdom and doing what God wants. Then all these other things you need will be given to you.

Matthew 6:33 NCV

Face facts: your life is a series of choices. From the instant you wake up in the morning until the moment you nod off to sleep at night, you make countless decisions—decisions about the things you do, decisions about the words you speak, and decisions about the way that you choose to direct your thoughts.

As a believer who has been transformed by the love of Jesus, you have every reason to make wise choices. But sometimes, when the daily grind threatens to grind you up and spit you out, you may make choices that are displeasing to God. When you do, you'll pay a price because you'll forfeit the happiness and the peace that might otherwise have been yours.

So, as you pause to consider the kind of Christian you are—and the kind of Christian you want to become—ask yourself whether you're sitting on the fence or standing in the light. The choice is yours . . . and so are the consequences.

GOD, WORSHIP, AND MARRIAGE

We love Him because He first loved us.

1 John 4:19 NKJV

When you and your spouse worship God together, you'll soon notice a change in your relationship. When the two of you sincerely embrace God's love, you will feel differently about yourself, your marriage, your family, and your world. When you and your spouse embrace God's love together, your marriage will be transformed. And, when the two of you accept the Father's grace and share His love, you will be blessed here on earth and throughout eternity.

So, if you genuinely seek to build a marriage that will stand the test of time, make God the centerpiece. When you do, your love will endure for a lifetime and beyond.

In order to be rightly oriented to God and His work, you need a God-centered life.

Henry Blackaby and Claude King

You get married not to be happy but to make each other happy.

Roy L. Smith

COMPASSIONATE SERVANTS

Finally, all of you be of one mind, having compassion for one another; love as brothers, be tenderhearted, be courteous.

1 Peter 3:8 NKJV

Concentration camp survivor Corrie ten Boom correctly observed, "The measure of a life is not its duration but its donation." These words remind us that the quality of our lives is determined not by what are able to take from others, but instead by what we are able to share with others.

God's Word commands us to be compassionate, generous servants to those who need our support. As believers, we have been richly blessed by our Creator. We, in turn, are called to share our gifts, our possessions, our testimonies, and our talents.

The thread of compassion is woven into the very fabric of Christ's teachings. If we are to be disciples of Christ, we, too, must be zealous in caring for others. Our Savior expects no less from us. And He deserves no less.

Carve your name on hearts, not on marble.

C. H. Spurgeon

CRITICS BEWARE

Don't pick on people, jump on their failures, criticize their faults—unless, of course, you want the same treatment. Don't condemn those who are down; that hardness can boomerang. Be easy on people; you'll find life a lot easier.

Luke 6:37 MSG

From experience, we know that it is easier to criticize than to correct. And we know that it is easier to find faults than solutions. Yet the urge to criticize others remains a powerful temptation for most of us. Our task, as obedient believers, is to break the twin habits of negative thinking and critical speech.

Negativity is highly contagious: we give it to others who, in turn, give it back to us. This cycle can be broken by positive thoughts, heartfelt prayers, and encouraging words. As thoughtful servants of a loving God, we can use the transforming power of Christ's love to break the chains of negativity. And we should.

Being critical of others, including God, is one way we try to avoid facing and judging our own sins.

Warren Wiersbe

WHEN PEOPLE BEHAVE BADLY

Bad temper is contagious—don't get infected.

Proverbs 22:25 MSG

Face it: sometimes people can be rude . . . very rude. When other people are unkind to you, you may be tempted to strike back, either verbally or in some other way. Don't do it! Instead, remember that God corrects other people's behaviors in His own way, and He doesn't need your help (even if you're totally convinced that He does).

So, when other people behave cruelly, foolishly, or impulsively—as they will from time to time—don't be hotheaded. Instead, speak up for yourself as politely as you can, and walk away. Then, forgive everybody as quickly as you can, and leave the rest up to God.

Turn your attention upon yourself and beware of judging the deeds of other men, for in judging others a man labors vainly, often makes mistakes, and easily sins; whereas, in judging and taking stock of himself he does something that is always profitable.

Thomas à Kempis

DOUBT AND THE TRUE BELIEVER

Immediately the father of the child cried out and said with tears, "Lord, I believe; help my unbelief!"

Mark 9:24 NKJV

If you've never had any doubts about your faith, then you can stop reading this page now and skip to the next. But if you've ever been plagued by doubts about your faith or your God, keep reading.

Even some of the most faithful Christians are, at times, beset by occasional bouts of discouragement and doubt. But even when we feel far removed from God, God is never far removed from us. He is always with us, always willing to calm the storms of life—always willing to replace our doubts with comfort and assurance.

Whenever you're plagued by doubts, that's precisely the moment you should seek God's presence by genuinely seeking to establish a deeper, more meaningful relationship with His Son. Then you may rest assured that in time, God will calm your fears, answer your prayers, and restore your confidence.

FOR ALL ETERNITY

Truly, truly, I say to you, he who hears My word, and believes Him who sent Me, has eternal life, and does not come into judgment, but has passed out of death into life. Truly, truly, I say to you, an hour is coming and now is, when the dead will hear the voice of the Son of God, and those who hear will live.

John 5:24-25 NASB

Your ability to envision the future, like your life here on earth, is limited. God's vision, however, is not burdened by any such limitations; He sees all things, He knows all things, and His plans for you endure for all time.

God's plans are not limited to the events of life here on earth. Your Heavenly Father has bigger things in mind for you . . . much bigger things. So praise the Creator for the gift of eternal life and share the Good News with all who cross your path. You have given your heart to the Son, so you belong to the Father—today, tomorrow, and for all eternity.

The choices of time are binding in eternity.

Jack MacArthur

A POSITIVE INFLUENCE

Be an example to the believers in word, in conduct, in love, in spirit, in faith, in purity.

1 Timothy 4:12 NKJV

As followers of Christ, we must each ask ourselves an important question: "What kind of example am I?" The answer to that question determines, in large part, whether or not we are positive influences on our own little corners of the world.

Are you the kind of man whose life serves as a powerful example of righteousness? Are you a person whose behavior serves as a positive role model for young people? Are you the kind of Christian whose actions, day in and day out, are based upon integrity, fidelity, and a love for the Lord? If so, you are not only blessed by God; you are also a powerful force for good in a world that desperately needs positive influences such as yours.

If you want your neighbor to know what Christ will do for him, let the neighbor see what Christ has done for you.

Henry Ward Beecher

TROUBLED TIMES

They won't be afraid of bad news; their hearts are steady because they trust the Lord.

Psalm 112:7 NCV

We live in a world that is, at times, a frightening place. We live in a world that is, at times, a discouraging place. We live in a world where life-changing losses can be so painful and so profound that it seems we will never recover. But, with God's help, and with the help of encouraging family members and friends, we can recover.

During the darker days of life, we are wise to remember the words of Jesus, who reassured His disciples, saying, "Take courage! It is I. Don't be afraid" (Matthew 14:27 NIV). Then, with God's comfort and His love in our hearts, we can offer encouragement to others. And by helping them face their fears, we can, in turn, tackle our own problems with courage, determination, and faith.

When we submit difficult and alarming situations to God, he promises that his peace will be like military garrison to guard our hearts from fear.

Dennis Swanberg

IN THE FOOTSTEPS OF JESUS

Whoever serves me must follow me. Then my servant will be with me everywhere I am. My Father will honor anyone who serves me.

John 12:26 NCV

Whom will you walk with today? Will you walk with people who worship the ways of the world? Or will you walk with the Son of God? Jesus walks with you. Are you walking with Him? Hopefully, you will choose to walk with Him today and every day of your life. God's Word promises that when you follow in Christ's footsteps, you will learn how to live freely and lightly (Matthew 11:28-30).

Are you worried about the day ahead? Be confident in God's power. He will never desert you. Are you concerned about the future? Be courageous and call upon God. He will protect you. Are you confused? Listen to the quiet voice of your Heavenly Father. He is not a God of confusion. So talk with God; listen to Him; and walk with His Son—starting now.

Christ is not valued at all unless He is valued above all.

St. Augustine

ALWAYS FORGIVING

Then Peter came to him and asked, "Lord, how often should I forgive someone who sins against me? Seven times?" "No!" Jesus replied, "seventy times seven!"

Matthew 18:21-22 NLT

How often should we forgive other people? More times than we can count (Matthew 18:21-22). That's a mighty tall order, but we must remember that it's an order from God—an order that must be obeyed.

In God's curriculum, forgiveness isn't optional; it's a required course. Sometimes, of course, we have a very difficult time forgiving the people who have hurt us, but if we don't find it in our hearts to forgive them, we not only hurt ourselves, we also disobey our Father in heaven. So we must forgive—and keep forgiving—as long as we live.

Doing an injury puts you below your enemy; revenging an injury makes you even with him; forgiving an injury sets you above him!

Anonymous

A TERRIFIC TOMORROW

"I say this because I know what I am planning for you," says the Lord. "I have good plans for you, not plans to hurt you. I will give you hope and a good future."

Jeremiah 29:11 NCV

Life is like a garden. Every day, God gives us opportunities to plant seeds for the future. When we plant wisely and trust God completely, the harvest is bountiful.

Are you willing to place your future in the hands of a loving and all-knowing God? Do you trust in the ultimate goodness of His plan for your life? Will you face today's challenges with optimism and hope? You should. After all, God created you for a very important reason: His reason. And you still have important work to do: His work.

Today, as you live in the present and look to the future, remember that God has a plan for you. Act—and believe—accordingly.

Those who keep speaking about the sun while walking under a cloudy sky are messengers of hope, the true saints of our day.

Henri Nouwen

OFFERING THANKS

In everything give thanks; for this is the will of God in Christ Jesus for you.

1 Thessalonians 5:18 NKJV

Sometimes, life here on earth can be complicated, demanding, and frustrating. When the demands of life leave us rushing from place to place with scarcely a moment to spare, we may fail to pause and thank our Creator for His gifts. But, whenever we neglect to give proper thanks to the Father, we suffer because of our misplaced priorities.

Today, begin making a list of your blessings. You most certainly will not be able to make a complete list, but take a few moments and jot down as many blessings as you can. Then, give thanks to the Giver of all good things: God. His love for you is eternal, as are His gifts. And it's never too soon—or too late—to offer Him thanks.

It is only with gratitude that life becomes rich.

Dietrich Bonhoeffer

TRANSCENDENT LOVE

Who will separate us from the love of Christ? Will tribulation, or distress, or persecution, or famine, or nakedness, or peril, or sword? But in all these things we overwhelmingly conquer through Him who loved us.

Romans 8:35, 37 NASB

Where can we find God's love? Everywhere. God's love transcends space and time. It reaches beyond the heavens, and it touches the darkest, smallest corner of every human heart. When we become passionate in our devotion to the Father, when we sincerely open our minds and hearts to Him, His love does not arrive "some day"—it arrives immediately.

Today, take God at His word and welcome His Son into your heart. When you do, God's transcendent love will surround you and transform you, now and forever.

The grace of God transcends all our feeble efforts to describe it. It cannot be poured into any mental receptacle without running over.

Vance Havner

HE REIGNS

In all your ways acknowledge Him, and He shall direct your paths.

Proverbs 3:6 NKJV

God is sovereign. He reigns over the entire universe, and He reigns over your little corner of that universe. Your challenge is to recognize God's sovereignty and live in accordance with His commandments. Sometimes, of course, this is easier said than done.

Your Heavenly Father may not always reveal Himself as quickly (or as clearly) as you would like. But rest assured: God is in control, God is here, and God intends to use you in wonderful, unexpected ways. He desires to lead you along a path of His choosing. Your challenge is to watch, to listen, to learn . . . and to follow.

He proves His sovereignty, not by intervening constantly and preventing these events, but by ruling and overruling them so that even tragedies end up accomplishing His ultimate purposes.

Warren Wiersbe

SEEKING HIS WILL

Teach me to do Your will, for You are my God; Your Spirit is good. Lead me in the land of uprightness.

Psalm 143:10 NKJV

God has a plan for our world and our lives. God does not do things by accident; He is willful and intentional. Unfortunately for us, we cannot always understand the will of God. Why? Because we are mortal beings with limited understanding. Although we cannot fully comprehend the will of God, we should always trust the will of God.

As this day unfolds, seek God's will and obey His Word. When you entrust your life to Him without reservation, He will give you the courage to meet any challenge, the strength to endure any trial, and the wisdom to live in His righteousness and in His peace.

"If the Lord will" is not just a statement on a believer's lips; it is the constant attitude of his heart.

Warren Wiersbe

There will be times when God's behavior will be incomprehensible and confusing to us.

James Dobson

A HELPING HAND

Then a Samaritan traveling down the road came to where the hurt man was. When he saw the man, he felt very sorry for him. The Samaritan went to him, poured olive oil and wine on his wounds, and bandaged them. Then he put the hurt man on his own donkey and took him to an inn where he cared for him.

Luke 10:33-34 NCV

Sometimes we would like to help make the world a better place, but we're not sure how to do it. Jesus told the story of the "Good Samaritan," a man who helped a fellow traveler when no one else would. We, too, should be good Samaritans when we find people who need our help.

When bad things happen in our world, there's always something we can do. So what can you do to make God's world a better place? You can start by making your own corner of the world a little nicer place to live (by sharing kind words and good deeds). And then, you can take your concerns to God in prayer. Whether you've offered a helping hand or a heartfelt prayer, you've done a lot.

LOOK BEFORE YOU LEAP

An impulsive vow is a trap; later you'll wish you could get out of it.

Proverbs 20:25 MSG

Are you, at times, just a little bit impulsive? Do you sometimes look before you leap? If so, God wants to have a little chat with you.

God's Word is clear: as believers, we are called to lead lives of discipline, diligence, moderation, and maturity. But the world often tempts us to behave otherwise. Everywhere we turn, or so it seems, we are faced with powerful temptations to behave in undisciplined, ungodly ways.

God's Word instructs us to be disciplined in our thoughts and our actions; God's Word warns us against the dangers of impulsive behavior. As believers in a just God, we should act and react accordingly.

Zeal without knowledge is always less useful and effective than regulated zeal, and very often is highly dangerous.

St. Bernard of Clairvaux

NEVER-ENDING LOVE

And he has given us this command: Whoever loves God must also love his brother.

1 John 4:21 NIV

C. S. Lewis observed, "A man's spiritual health is exactly proportional to his love for God." If we are to enjoy the spiritual health that God intends for us, we must praise Him, we must love Him, and we must obey Him.

When we worship God faithfully and obediently, we invite His love into our hearts. When we truly worship God, we allow Him to rule over our days and our lives. In turn, we grow to love God even more deeply as we sense His love for us.

Today, open your heart to the Father. And let your obedience be a fitting response to His never-ending love.

The only true source of meaning in life is found in love for God and his son Jesus Christ, and love for mankind, beginning with our own families.

James Dobson

DREAM BIG

With God's power working in us, God can do much, much more than anything we can ask or imagine.

Ephesians 3:20 NCV

Are you willing to entertain the possibility that God has big plans in store for you? Hopefully so. Yet sometimes, especially if you've recently experienced a life-altering disappointment, you may find it difficult to envision a brighter future for yourself and your family. If so, it's time to reconsider your own capabilities . . . and God's.

Your Heavenly Father created you with unique gifts and untapped talents; your job is to tap them. When you do, you'll begin to feel an increasing sense of confidence in yourself and in your future. So even if you're experiencing difficult days, don't abandon your dreams. Instead, trust that God is preparing you for greater things.

When you affirm big, believe big, and pray big, big things happen.

Norman Vincent Peale

Dreaming the dream of God is not for cowards.

Joey Johnson

HOPE IS CONTAGIOUS

Finally, all of you be of one mind, having compassion for one another; love as brothers, be tenderhearted, be courteous.

1 Peter 3:8 NKJV

One of the reasons that God placed you here on earth is so that you might become a beacon of encouragement to the world. As a faithful follower of the One from Galilee, you have every reason to be hopeful, and you have every reason to share your hopes with others. When you do, you will discover that hope, like other human emotions, is contagious.

As a follower of Christ, you are instructed to choose your words carefully so as to build others up through wholesome, honest encouragement (Ephesians 4:29). So look for the good in others and celebrate the good that you find. As the old saying goes, "When someone does something good, applaud—you'll make two people happy."

There are no words to express the abyss between isolation and having one ally. It may be conceded to the mathematician that four is twice two. But, two is not twice one; two is two thousand times one.

G. K. Chesterton

HOW TO TREAT OTHERS: A SIMPLE RULE OF THUMB

Here is a simple, rule-of-thumb for behavior: Ask yourself what you want people to do for you, then grab the initiative and do it for them. Add up God's Law and Prophets and this is what you get.

Matthew 7:12 MSG

Would you like to make the world a better place? If so, you can start by practicing the Golden Rule.

Is the Golden Rule your rule, or is it just another Bible verse that goes in one ear and out the other? Jesus made Himself perfectly clear: He instructed you to treat other people in the same way that you want to be treated. But sometimes, especially when you're feeling the pressures of everyday living, obeying the Golden Rule can seem like an impossible task—but it's not. So if you want to know how to treat other people, ask the person you see every time you look into the mirror. The answer you receive will tell you exactly what to do.

It is wrong for anyone to be anxious to receive more from his neighbor than he himself is willing to give to God.

St. Francis of Assisi

HIS HEALING TOUCH

I am the L*ORD that healeth thee.*

Exodus 15:26 KJV

Are you concerned about your spiritual, physical, or emotional health? If so, there is a timeless source of comfort and assurance that is as near as your bookshelf. That source is the Holy Bible.

God's Word has much to say about every aspect of your life, including your health. And, when you face concerns of any sort—including health-related challenges—God is with you. So trust your medical doctor to do his or her part, but place your ultimate trust in your benevolent Heavenly Father. His healing touch, like His love, endures forever.

The healing acts of Jesus were themselves a message that he had come to set men free.

Francis MacNutt

Jesus Christ is the One by Whom, for Whom, through Whom everything was made. Therefore, He knows what's wrong in your life and how to fix it.

Anne Graham Lotz

THE BEST POLICY

The godly are directed by their honesty.

Proverbs 11:5 NLT

From the time we are children, we are taught that honesty is the best policy, but sometimes, being honest is hard. So, we convince ourselves that it's all right to tell "little white lies." But there's a problem: Little white lies tend to grow up, and when they do, they cause havoc and pain in our lives.

For Christians, the issue of honesty is not a topic for debate. Honesty is not just the best policy; it is God's policy, pure and simple. And if we are to be servants worthy of our Savior, Jesus Christ, we must avoid all lies, white or otherwise. So, if you're tempted to sow the seeds of deception (perhaps in the form of a "harmless" white lie), resist that temptation. Truth is God's way, and a lie—of whatever color—is not.

God doesn't expect you to be perfect, but he does insist on complete honesty.

Rick Warren

Falsehood is cowardice, the truth courage.

Hosea Ballou

GOD'S LESSONS

Take good counsel and accept correction—that's the way to live wisely and well.

Proverbs 19:20 MSG

When it comes to learning life's lessons, we can either do things the easy way or the hard way. The easy way can be summed up as follows: when God teaches us a lesson, we learn it . . . the first time! Unfortunately, too many of us learn much more slowly than that.

When we resist God's instruction, He continues to teach, whether we like it or not. Our challenge, then, is to discern God's lessons from the experiences of everyday life. Hopefully, we learn those lessons sooner rather than later because the sooner we do, the sooner He can move on to the next lesson and the next, and the next.

The wise man gives proper appreciation in his life to this past. He learns to sift the sawdust of heritage in order to find the nuggets that make the current moment have any meaning.

Grady Nutt

TOO MANY POSSESSIONS

Love not the world, neither the things that are in the world. If any man love the world, the love of the Father is not in him.

1 John 2:15 KJV

On the grand stage of a well-lived life, material possessions should play a rather small role. Of course, we all need the basic necessities of life, but once we meet those needs for ourselves and for our families, the piling up of possessions creates more problems than it solves. Our real riches, of course, are not of this world. We are never really rich until we are rich in spirit.

How much stuff is too much stuff? Well, if your desire for stuff is getting in the way of your desire to know God, then you've got too much stuff—it's as simple as that. So, if you find yourself wrapped up in the concerns of the material world, it's time to reorder your priorities. And, it's time to begin storing up riches that will endure throughout eternity—the spiritual kind.

Greed is evil because it substitutes material things for the place of honor that the Creator ought to have in an individual's life.

Charles Stanley

ON BEING AN OPTIMISTIC CHRISTIAN

Make me hear joy and gladness.

Psalm 51:8 NKJV

To be a pessimistic Christian is a contradiction in terms, yet sometimes even the most devout Christians fall prey to fear, doubt, and discouragement. But, God has a different plan for our lives. The comforting words of the 23rd Psalm remind us of God's blessings. In response to His grace, we should strive to focus our thoughts on things that are pleasing to Him, not upon things that are evil, discouraging, or frustrating.

So, the next time you find yourself mired in the pit of pessimism, remember God's Word and redirect your thoughts. This world is God's creation; look for the best in it, and trust Him to take care of the rest.

Great hopes make great men.

Thomas Fuller

Hope is some extraordinary spiritual grace that God gives us to control our fears, not to oust them.

Vincent McNabb

A WING AND A PRAYER

Be cheerful. Keep things in good repair. Keep your spirits up. Think in harmony. Be agreeable. Do all that, and the God of love and peace will be with you for sure.

2 Corinthians 13:11 MSG

Mrs. Charles E. Cowman, the author of the classic devotional text, *Streams in the Desert*, wrote, "Two wings are necessary to lift our souls toward God: prayer and praise. Prayer asks. Praise accepts the answer." That's why we should find the time to lift our concerns to God in prayer, and to praise Him for all that He has done.

John Wesley correctly observed, "Sour godliness is the devil's religion." These words remind us that pessimism and doubt are some of the most important tools that Satan uses to achieve his objectives. Our challenge, of course, is to ensure that Satan cannot use these tools on us.

Are you a cheerful Christian? You should be! And what is the best way to attain the joy that is rightfully yours? By giving Christ what is rightfully His: your heart, your soul, and your life.

GOD IS HERE

Draw near to God, and He will draw near to you.

James 4:8 HCSB

God is constantly making Himself available to you; therefore, when you approach Him obediently and sincerely, You will most certainly find Him: God is always available to you. Whenever it seems to you that God is distant, disinterested, or altogether absent, you may rest assured that your feelings are a reflection of your own emotional state, not an indication of God's absence.

If, during life's darker days, you seek to establish a closer relationship with Him, you can do so because God is not just near, He is here.

What is it that keeps me and you close to God in the good times? It is in solitude, quietness, waiting, and listening. It is seeking before anything and everything the face and the voice of God.

Ronald E. Wilson

KEEP POSSESSIONS IN PERSPECTIVE

A man's life does not consist in the abundance of his possessions.

Luke 12:15 NIV

All too often, we focus our thoughts and energies on the accumulation of earthly treasures, leaving precious little time to accumulate the only treasures that really matter: the spiritual kind. Our material possessions have the potential to do great good or terrible harm, depending upon how we choose to use them. As believers, our instructions are clear: we must use our possessions in accordance with God's commandments, and we must be faithful stewards of the gifts He has seen fit to bestow upon us.

Today, let us honor God by placing no other gods before Him. God comes first; everything else comes next—and "everything else" most certainly includes all of our earthly possessions.

If you want to be truly happy, you won't find it on an endless quest for more stuff. You'll find it in receiving God's generosity and in passing that generosity along.

Bill Hybels

HE RENEWS OUR STRENGTH

Do you not know? Have you not heard? The Everlasting God, the LORD, the Creator of the ends of the earth does not become weary or tired. His understanding is inscrutable. He gives strength to the weary, and to him who lacks might He increases power.

Isaiah 40:28–29 NASB

When we genuinely lift our hearts and prayers to God, He renews our strength. Are you almost too weary to lift your head? Then bow it. Offer your concerns and your fears to your Father in heaven. He is always at your side, offering His love and His strength.

Are you troubled or anxious? Take your anxieties to God in prayer. Are you weak or worried? Delve deeply into God's Holy Word and sense His presence in the quiet moments of the day. Are you spiritually exhausted? Call upon fellow believers to support you, and call upon Christ to renew your spirit and your life. Your Savior will never let you down. To the contrary, He will always lift you up if you ask Him to. So what, dear friend, are you waiting for?

A PASSIONATE PURSUIT OF GOD'S TRUTH

But grow in the grace and knowledge of our Lord and Savior Jesus Christ. To Him be the glory both now and forever. Amen.

2 Peter 3:18 NKJV

Have you established a passionate relationship with God's Holy Word? Hopefully so. The words of Matthew 4:4 remind us that, "Man shall not live by bread alone but by every word that proceedeth out of the mouth of God" (KJV). As believers, we must study the Bible and meditate upon its meaning for our lives. Otherwise, we deprive ourselves of a priceless gift from our Creator.

Martin Luther observed, "The Bible is alive, it speaks to me; it has feet, it runs after me; it has hands, it lays hold of me. The Bible is not antique or modern. It is eternal." God's Holy Word is, indeed, an eternal, transforming, one-of-a-kind treasure. And, a passing acquaintance with the Good Book is insufficient for Christians who seek to obey God's Word and to understand His will—passionate believers must never live by bread alone . . . .

COMMISSIONED TO WITNESS

Therefore go and make disciples of all nations, baptizing them in the name of the Father and of the Son and of the Holy Spirit, and teaching them to obey everything I have commanded you. And surely I am with you always, to the very end of the age.

Matthew 28:19-20 NIV

After His resurrection, Jesus addressed His disciples. As recorded in the 28th chapter of Matthew, Christ instructed His followers to share His message with the world. This "Great Commission" applies to Christians of every generation, including our own.

As believers, we are called to share the Good News of Jesus with our families, with our neighbors, and with the world. Christ commanded His disciples to become fishers of men. We must do likewise, and we must do so today. Tomorrow may indeed be too late.

Witnessing is not something that we do for the Lord; it is something that He does through us if we are filled with the Holy Spirit.

Warren Wiersbe

SHARING THE GOOD NEWS

Christ did not send me to baptize people but to preach the Good News. And he sent me to preach the Good News without using words of human wisdom so that the cross of Christ would not lose its power.

1 Corinthians 1:17 NCV

In his second letter to Timothy, Paul offers a message to believers of every generation when he writes, "God has not given us a spirit of timidity" (1:7 NASB). Paul's meaning is crystal clear: When sharing our testimonies, we, as Christians, must be courageous, forthright, and unashamed.

We live in a world that desperately needs the healing message of Christ Jesus. Every believer, each in his or her own way, bears a personal responsibility for sharing that message. If you are a believer in Christ, you know how He has touched your heart and changed your life. Now it's your turn to share the Good News with others. And remember: today is the perfect time to share your testimony because tomorrow may quite simply be too late.

To stand in an uncaring world and say, "See, here is the Christ" is a daring act of courage.

Calvin Miller

THE TRAP OF ADDICTION

Therefore submit to God. Resist the devil and he will flee from you. Draw near to God and He will draw near to you. Cleanse your hands, you sinners; and purify your hearts, you double-minded.

James 4:7-8 NKJV

The dictionary defines *addiction* as "the compulsive need for a habit-forming substance; the condition of being habitually and compulsively occupied with something." That definition is accurate but incomplete. For Christians, addiction has an additional meaning; it means compulsively worshipping something other than God.

Unless you're living on a deserted island, you know people who are full-blown addicts—probably lots of people. If you, or someone you love, is suffering from the blight of addiction, remember this: Help is available.

And if you're one of those fortunate people who has never experimented with addictive substances, congratulations. You just have spared yourself a lifetime of headaches and heartaches.

We are meant to be addicted to God, but we develop secondary addictions that temporarily appear to fix our problems.

Edward M. Berckman

FORGIVENESS AT HOME

Let all bitterness, wrath, anger, clamor, and evil speaking be put away from you, with all malice. And be kind to one another, tenderhearted, forgiving one another, just as God in Christ forgave you.

Ephesians 4:31-32 NKJV

Sometimes, it's easy to become angry with the people we love most, and sometimes it's hard to forgive them. After all, we know that our family will still love us no matter how angry we become. But while it's easy to become angry at home, it's usually wrong.

The next time you're tempted to lose your temper or to remain angry at a close family member, ask God to help you find the wisdom to forgive. And while you're at it, do your best to calm down sooner rather than later because peace is always beautiful, especially when it's peace at your house.

The fire of anger, if not quenched by loving forgiveness, will spread and defile and destroy the work of God.

Warren Wiersbe

THE DIRECTION OF YOUR THOUGHTS

My cup runs over. Surely goodness and mercy shall follow me all the days of my life; and I will dwell in the house of the LORD Forever.

Psalm 23:5-6 NKJV

God has given you free will, including the ability to influence the direction and the tone of your thoughts. And, here's how God wants you to direct those thoughts: "Finally brothers, whatever is true, whatever is honorable, whatever is just, whatever is pure, whatever is lovely, whatever is commendable—if there is any moral excellence and if there is any praise—dwell on these things" (Philippians 4:8 HCSB).

The quality of your attitude will help determine the quality of your life, so you must guard your thoughts accordingly. So, the next time you find yourself dwelling upon the negative aspects of your life, refocus your attention on things positive. And, the next time you're tempted to waste valuable time gossiping or complaining, resist those temptations with all your might. And remember: You'll never whine your way to the top . . . so don't waste your breath.

WHEN ANGER IS OKAY

The face of the LORD is against those who do evil.

Psalm 34:16 NKJV

Sometimes, anger can be a good thing. In the 22nd chapter of Matthew, we see how Christ responded when He confronted the evildoings of those who invaded His Father's house of worship: "And Jesus entered the temple and drove out all those who were buying and selling in the temple, and overturned the tables of the moneychangers and the seats of those who were selling doves" (v. 12 NASB). Thus, Jesus proved that righteous indignation is an appropriate response to evil.

When you come face-to-face with the devil's handiwork, don't be satisfied to remain safely on the sidelines. Instead, follow in the footsteps of your Savior. Jesus never compromised with evil, and neither should you.

There is a holy anger, excited by zeal, that moves us to reprove with warmth those whom our mildness failed to correct.

Jean Baptiste de la Salle

IN HIS IMAGE

So God created man in his own image, in the image of God he created him; male and female he created them.

Genesis 1:27 NIV

What is your attitude today? Are you fearful or worried? Are you more concerned about pleasing your friends than about pleasing your God? Are you bitter, confused, cynical or pessimistic? If so, it's time to have a little chat with your Father in heaven.

God intends that your life be filled with spiritual abundance and joy—but God will not force His joy upon you—you must claim it for yourself. So do yourself this favor: accept God's gifts with a smile on your face, a song on your lips, and joy in your heart. Think optimistically about yourself and your future. Give thanks to the One who has given you everything, and trust in your heart that He wants to give you so much more.

Our attitude determines our approach to life.

John Maxwell

WHAT DOES YOUR BEHAVIOR SAY ABOUT YOU?

As you have therefore received Christ Jesus the Lord, so walk in Him, rooted and built up in Him and established in the faith, as you have been taught, abounding in it with thanksgiving.

Colossians 2:6-7 NKJV

As Christians, we must do our best to make sure that our actions are accurate reflections of our beliefs. Our theology must be demonstrated, not only by our words but, more importantly, by our actions. In short, we should be practical believers, quick to act whenever we see an opportunity to serve God.

English clergyman Thomas Fuller observed, "He does not believe who does not live according to his beliefs." These words are most certainly true. Whether you like it or not, your life is an accurate reflection of your creed. If this fact gives you cause for concern, don't bother talking about the changes that you intend to make—make them. And then, when your good deeds speak for themselves—as they most certainly will—don't interrupt.

Obedience is the natural outcome of belief.

C. H. Spurgeon

REJOICE!

Rejoice in the Lord always. Again I will say, rejoice!

Philippians 4:4 NKJV

Are you living a life of agitation, consternation, or celebration? If you're a believer, it should most certainly be the latter. With Christ as your Savior, every day should be a time of celebration.

Oswald Chambers correctly observed, "Joy is the great note all throughout the Bible." C. S. Lewis echoed that thought when he wrote, "Joy is the serious business of heaven." But, even the most dedicated Christians can, on occasion, forget to celebrate each day for what it is: a priceless gift from God.

Today, celebrate the life that God has given you. Today, put a smile on your face, kind words on your lips, and a song in your heart. Be generous with your praise and free with your encouragement. And then, when you have celebrated life to the fullest, invite your friends to do likewise. After all, this is God's day, and He has given us clear instructions for its use. We are commanded to rejoice and be glad. So, with no further ado, let the celebration begin . . .

THE GIFT OF CHEERFULNESS

Worry is a heavy load, but a kind word cheers you up.

Proverbs 12:25 NCV

Cheerfulness is a gift that we give to others and to ourselves. And, as believers who have been saved by a risen Christ, why shouldn't we be cheerful? The answer, of course, is that we have every reason to honor our Savior with joy in our hearts, smiles on our faces, and words of celebration on our lips.

Christ promises us lives of abundance and joy if we accept His love and His grace. Yet sometimes, even the most righteous among us are beset by fits of ill temper and frustration. During these moments, we may not feel like turning our thoughts and prayers to Christ, but that's precisely what we should do. When we do so, we simply can't stay grumpy for long.

When I think of God, my heart is so full of joy that the notes leap and dance as they leave my pen; and since God has given me a cheerful heart, I serve him with a cheerful spirit.

Franz Joseph Haydn

OBEDIENCE NOW

By this we know that we have come to know Him, if we keep His commandments.

1 John 2:3 NASB

In order to enjoy a deeper relationship with God, you must strive diligently to live in accordance with His commandments. But there's a problem—you live in a world that seeks to snare your attention and lead you away from God.

Because you are an imperfect mortal being, you cannot be perfectly obedient, nor does God expect you to be. What is required, however, is a sincere desire to be obedient coupled with an awareness of sin and a willingness to distance yourself from it as soon as you encounter it.

Are you willing to conform your behavior to God's rules? Hopefully, you can answer that question with a resounding yes. Otherwise, you'll never experience a full measure of the blessings that the Creator gives to those who obey Him.

We grow spiritually as our Lord grew physically: by a life of simple, unobtrusive obedience.

Oswald Chambers

BUILDING HIS CHURCH

For we are God's fellow workers; you are God's field, you are God's building.

1 Corinthians 3:9 NKJV

In the Book of Acts, Luke reminds us to "feed the church of God" (20:28). As Christians who have been saved by a loving, compassionate Creator, we are compelled not only to worship Him in our hearts but also to worship Him in the presence of fellow believers.

The church belongs to God; it is His just as certainly as we are His. When we help build God's church, we bear witness to the changes that He has made in our lives.

Today and every day, let us worship God with grateful hearts and helping hands as we support the church that He has created. Let us witness to our friends, to our families, and to the world. When we do so, we bless others and we are blessed by the One who sent His Son to die so that we might have eternal life.

Only participation in the full life of a local church builds spiritual muscle.

Rick Warren

FINDING CONTENTMENT

I've learned by now to be quite content whatever my circumstances. I'm just as happy with little as with much, with much as with little. I've found the recipe for being happy whether full or hungry, hands full or hands empty.

Philippians 4:11-12 MSG

Where can we find contentment? Is it a result of wealth or power or beauty or fame? Hardly. Genuine contentment is a gift from God to those who trust Him and follow His commandments.

Our modern world seems preoccupied with the search for happiness. We are bombarded with messages telling us that happiness depends upon the acquisition of material possessions. These messages are false. Enduring peace is not the result of our acquisitions; it is a spiritual gift from God to those who obey Him and accept His will.

If we don't find contentment in God, we will never find it anywhere else. But, if we seek Him and obey Him, we will be blessed with an inner peace that is beyond human understanding. When God dwells at the center of our lives, peace and contentment will belong to us just as surely as we belong to God.

PROTECTED

Be of good courage, And He shall strengthen your heart, All you who hope in the LORD.

Psalm 31:24 NKJV

Being a godly man in this difficult world is no easy task. Ours is a time of uncertainty and danger, a time when even the most courageous have legitimate cause for concern. But as believers we can live courageously, knowing that we have been saved by a loving Father and His only begotten Son.

Are you anxious? Take those anxieties to God. Are you troubled? Take your troubles to Him. Seek protection from the One who cannot be moved. And then live courageously, knowing that even in these troubled times, God is always as near as your next breath—and you are always protected.

A man who is intimate with God will never be intimidated by men.

Leonard Ravenhill

The task ahead of us is never as great as the Power behind us.

Anonymous

DEALING WITH DISAPPOINTMENT

But this happened so we would not trust in ourselves but in God, who raises people from the dead. God saved us from these great dangers of death, and he will continue to save us. We have put our hope in him, and he will save us again.

2 *Corinthians* 1:9-10 NCV

From time to time, all of us face life-altering disappointments that leave us breathless. Oftentimes, these disappointments come unexpectedly, leaving us with more questions than answers. But even when we don't have all the answers—or, for that matter, even when we don't seem to have any of the answers—God does. Whatever our circumstances, whether we stand atop the highest mountain or wander through the darkest valley, God is ready to protect us, to comfort us, and to heal us. Our task is to let Him.

The next time you're disappointed, don't panic and don't give up. Just be patient and let God remind you he's still in control.

Max Lucado

THY WILL BE DONE

"Father, if it is Your will, take this cup away from Me; nevertheless not My will, but Yours, be done."

Luke 22:42 NKJV

As human beings with limited understanding, we can never fully comprehend the will of God. But as believers in a benevolent God, we must always trust the will of our Heavenly Father.

Before His crucifixion, Jesus went to the Mount of Olives and poured out His heart to God. Jesus knew of the agony that He was destined to endure, but He also knew that God's will must be done. We, like our Savior, face trials that bring fear and trembling to the very depths of our souls, but like Christ, we, too, must ultimately seek God's will, not our own. When we entrust our lives to Him completely and without reservation, He gives us the strength to meet any challenge, the courage to face any trial, and the wisdom to live in His righteousness.

To know the will of God is the greatest knowledge! To do the will of God is the greatest achievement.

George W. Truett

ABANDONING BAD HABITS

Do not be deceived: "Evil company corrupts good habits."

1 Corinthians 15:33 NKJV

It's an old saying and a true one: First, you make your habits, and then your habits make you. Some habits will inevitably bring you closer to God; other habits will lead you away from the path He has chosen for you. If you sincerely desire to improve your spiritual health, you must honestly examine the habits that make up the fabric of your day. And you must abandon those habits that are displeasing to God.

If you trust God, and if you keep asking for His help, He can transform your life. If you sincerely ask Him to help you, the same God who created the universe will help you defeat the harmful habits that have heretofore defeated you. So, if at first you don't succeed, keep praying. God is listening, and He's ready to help you become a better person if you ask Him . . . so ask today.

If you do not shun small defects, bit by bit you will fall into greater ones.

Thomas à Kempis

FINDING HOPE

These things I have spoken to you, that in Me you may have peace. In the world you will have tribulation; but be of good cheer, I have overcome the world.

John 16:33 NKJV

There are few sadder sights on earth than the sight of a person who has lost all hope. In difficult times, hope can be elusive, but Christians need never lose it. After all, God is good; His love endures; He has promised His children the gift of eternal life.

If you find yourself falling into the spiritual traps of worry and discouragement, consider the words of Jesus. It was Christ who promised, "In the world you will have tribulation; but be of good cheer, I have overcome the world." This world is indeed a place of trials and tribulations, but as believers, we are secure. God has promised us peace, joy, and eternal life. And, of course, God always keeps His promises.

God is the only one who can make the valley of trouble a door of hope.

Catherine Marshall

TO JUDGE OR NOT TO JUDGE

When they continued to ask Jesus their question, he raised up and said, "Anyone here who has never sinned can throw the first stone at her."

John 8:7 NCV

The warning of Matthew 7:1 is clear: "Judge not, that ye be not judged" (KJV). Yet even the most devoted Christians may fall prey to a powerful yet subtle temptation: the temptation to judge others. But as obedient followers of Christ, we are commanded to refrain from such behavior.

As Jesus came upon a young woman who had been condemned by the Pharisees, He spoke not only to the crowd that was gathered there, but also to all generations when He warned, "He that is without sin among you, let him first cast a stone at her" (John 8:7 KJV). Christ's message is clear, and it applies not only to the Pharisees of ancient times, but also to us.

Being critical of others, including God, is one way we try to avoid facing and judging our own sins.

Warren Wiersbe

THE WORLD . . . AND YOU

Don't copy the behavior and customs of this world, but let God transform you into a new person by changing the way you think.

Romans 12:2 NLT

We live in the world, but we must not worship it. Our duty is to place God first and everything else second. But because we are fallible beings with imperfect faith, placing God in His rightful place is often difficult. In fact, at every turn, or so it seems, we are tempted to do otherwise.

The 21st-century world is a noisy, distracting place filled with countless opportunities to stray from God's will. The world seems to cry, "Worship me with your time, your money, your energy, and your thoughts!" But God commands otherwise: He commands us to worship Him and Him alone; everything else must be secondary.

The only ultimate disaster that can befall us, I have come to realize, is to feel ourselves to be home on earth.

Max Lucado

THE LOVE OF MONEY

For the love of money is a root of all sorts of evil, and some by longing for it have wandered away from the faith and pierced themselves with many griefs.

1 Timothy 6:10 NASB

Earthly riches are temporary: here today and soon gone forever. Spiritual riches, on the other hand, are permanent: ours today, ours tomorrow, ours throughout eternity. Yet all too often, we focus our thoughts and energies on the accumulation of earthly treasures, leaving precious little time to accumulate the only treasures that really matter: the spiritual kind.

Our society is in love with money and the things that money can buy. God is not. God cares about people, not possessions, and so must we. We must, to the best of our abilities, love our neighbors as ourselves, and we must, to the best of our abilities, resist the mighty temptation to place possessions ahead of people.

Money, in and of itself, is not evil, but worshipping money is. So today, as you prioritize matters of importance for you and yours, remember that God is almighty, but the "almighty" dollar is not.

THE PRINCE OF PEACE

Peace I leave with you; My peace I give to you; not as the world gives do I give to you. Do not let your heart be troubled, nor let it be fearful.

John 14:27 NASB

Have you found the genuine peace that can be yours through Jesus Christ? Or are you still rushing after the illusion of "peace and happiness" that the world promises but cannot deliver? The beautiful words of John 14:27 remind us that Jesus offers us peace, not as the world gives, but as He alone gives. Our challenge is to accept Christ's peace into our hearts and then, as best we can, to share His peace with our neighbors.

Today, as a gift to yourself, to your family, and to your friends, claim the inner peace that is your spiritual birthright: the peace of Jesus Christ. It is offered freely; it has been paid for in full; it is yours for the asking. So ask. And then share.

The better acquainted you become with God, the less tensions you feel and the more peace you possess.

Charles Allen

CONSTANT PRAISE

Through Him then, let us continually offer up a sacrifice of praise to God, that is, the fruit of lips that give thanks to His name.

Hebrews 13:15 NASB

The Bible makes it clear: it pays to praise God. But sometimes, we allow ourselves to become so preoccupied with the demands of daily life that we forget to say "Thank You" to the Giver of all good gifts.

Worship and praise should be a part of everything we do. Otherwise, we quickly lose perspective as we fall prey to the demands of the moment.

Do you sincerely desire to be a worthy servant of the One who has given you eternal love and eternal life? Then praise Him for who He is and for what He has done for you. Praise Him all day long, every day, for as long as you live . . . and then for all eternity.

Praise God from whom all blessings flow. Praise Him all creatures here below. Praise Him above ye heavenly host. Praise Father, Son, and Holy Ghost.

Thomas Ken

A TIME TO REST

Come to me, all you who are weary and burdened, and I will give you rest. Take my yoke upon you and learn from me, for I am gentle and humble in heart, and you will find rest for your souls. For my yoke is easy and my burden is light.

Matthew 11:28-30 NIV

Sometimes, the struggles of life can drain us of our strength. When we find ourselves tired, discouraged, or worse, there is a source from which we can draw the power needed to recharge our spiritual batteries. That source, of course, is God.

God expects us to work hard, but He also intends for us to rest. When we fail to take the rest that we need, we do a disservice to ourselves and to our families.

Is your spiritual battery running low? Is your energy on the wane? Are your emotions frayed? If so, it's time to turn your thoughts and your prayers to God. And when you're finished, it's time to rest.

One reason so much American Christianity is a mile wide and an inch deep is that Christians are simply tired. Sometimes you need to kick back and rest for Jesus' sake.

Dennis Swanberg

THE SHEPHERD'S GIFT

My cup runs over. Surely goodness and mercy shall follow me all the days of my life; and I will dwell in the house of the LORD forever.

Psalm 23:5-6 NKJV

God's Word is clear: Christ came in order that we might have life abundant and life eternal. Eternal life is the priceless possession of all who invite Christ into their hearts, but God's abundance is optional: He does not force it upon us.

When we entrust our hearts and our days to the One who created us, we experience abundance through the grace and sacrifice of His Son. But, when we turn our thoughts and direct our energies away from God's commandments, we inevitably forfeit the spiritual abundance that might otherwise be ours.

Do you sincerely seek the riches that our Savior offers to those who give themselves to Him? Then follow Him completely and obey Him without reservation. When you do, you will receive the love and the abundance that He has promised. Seek first the salvation that is available through a personal relationship with Jesus Christ, and then claim the joy, the peace, and the spiritual abundance that the Shepherd offers His sheep.

FACE-TO-FACE WITH OLD MAN TROUBLE

When you go through deep waters and great trouble, I will be with you. When you go through the rivers of difficulty, you will not drown! When you walk through the fire of oppression, you will not be burned up; the flames will not consume you. For I am the LORD*, your God, the Holy One of Israel, your Savior.*

Isaiah 43:2-3 NLT

As life-here-on-earth unfolds, all of us encounter occasional setbacks: Those occasional visits from Old Man Trouble are simply a fact of life, and none of us are exempt. When tough times arrive, we may be forced to rearrange our plans and our priorities. But even on our darkest days, we must remember that God's love remains constant.

The fact that we encounter adversity is not nearly so important as the way we choose to deal with it. When tough times arrive, we have a clear choice: we can begin the difficult work of tackling our troubles . . . or not. When we summon the courage to look Old Man Trouble squarely in the eye, an amazing thing usually happens: he blinks.

KEEPING UP APPEARANCES

We justify our actions by appearances; God examines our motives.

Proverbs 21:2 MSG

The world sees you as you appear to be; God sees you as you really are . . . He sees your heart, and He understands your intentions. The opinions of others should be relatively unimportant to you; however, God's view of you—His understanding of your actions, your thoughts, and your motivations—should be vitally important.

Few things in life are more futile than "keeping up appearances" for the sake of neighbors. What is important, of course, is pleasing your Father in heaven. You please Him when your intentions are pure and your actions are just.

Outside appearances, things like the clothes you wear or the car you drive, are important to other people but totally unimportant to God. Trust God.

Marie T. Freeman

BELIEVING MAKES A DIFFERENCE

You love Him, though you have not seen Him. And though not seeing Him now, you believe in Him and rejoice with inexpressible and glorious joy, because you are receiving the goal of your faith, the salvation of your souls.

1 Peter 1:8-9 HCSB

If you'd like to partake in the peace that only God can give, make certain that your actions are guided by His Word. And while you're at it, pay careful attention to the conscience that God, in His infinite wisdom, has placed in your heart. Don't treat your faith as if it were separate from your everyday life. Weave your beliefs into the very fabric of your day. When you do, God will honor your good works, and your good works will honor God.

If you seek to be a responsible believer, you must realize that it is never enough to hear the instructions of God; you must also live by them. And it is never enough to wait idly by while others to do God's work here on earth; you, too, must act. Doing God's work is a responsibility that every Christian (including you) should bear. And when you do, your loving Heavenly Father will reward your efforts with a bountiful harvest.

THE FUTILITY OF BLAMING OTHERS

As He passed by, He saw a man blind from birth. And His disciples asked Him, "Rabbi, who sinned, this man or his parents, that he would be born blind?" Jesus answered, "It was neither that this man sinned, nor his parents; but it was so that the works of God might be displayed in him."

John 9:1-3 NASB

To blame others for our own problems is the height of futility. Yet blaming others is a favorite human pastime. Why? Because blaming is much easier than fixing, and criticizing others is so much easier than improving ourselves. So instead of solving our problems legitimately (by doing the work required to solve them), we are inclined to fret, to blame, and to criticize, while doing precious little else. When we do, our problems, quite predictably, remain unsolved.

So, instead of looking for someone to blame, look for something to fix, and then get busy fixing it. And as you consider your own situation, remember this: God has a way of helping those who help themselves, but He doesn't spend much time helping those who don't.

CHARACTER COUNTS

Applying all diligence, in your faith supply moral excellence.

2 Peter 1:5 NASB

Character is built slowly over a lifetime. It is the sum of every right decision, every honest word, every noble thought, and every heartfelt prayer. It is forged on the anvil of honorable work and polished by the twin virtues of generosity and humility. Character is a precious thing—difficult to build but easy to tear down. As believers in Christ, we must seek to live each day with discipline, honesty, and faith. When we do, integrity becomes a habit. And God smiles.

Character is formed by doing the thing we are supposed to do, when it should be done, whether we feel like doing it or not.

Father Flanagan

Integrity is the glue that holds our way of life together. We must constantly strive to keep our integrity intact. When wealth is lost, nothing is lost; when health is lost, something is lost; when character is lost, all is lost.

Billy Graham

CHOOSING WISELY

But the wisdom that is from above is first pure, then peaceable, gentle, willing to yield, full of mercy and good fruits, without partiality and without hypocrisy.

James 3:17 NKJV

Every life, including yours, is a tapestry of choices. And the quality of your life depends, to a surprising extent, on the quality of the choices you make.

Would you like to enjoy a life of abundance and significance? If so, you must you must make choices that are pleasing to God.

From the instant you wake up in the morning until the moment you nod off to sleep at night, you make lots of decisions: decisions about the things you do, decisions about the words you speak, and decisions about the thoughts you choose to think.

Today and every day, it's up to you (and only you) to make wise choices, choices that enhance your relationship with God. After all, He deserves no less than your best . . . and so do you.

God expresses His love in giving us the freedom to choose.

Charles Stanley

HIS POWER AND YOURS

When we were baptized, we were buried with Christ and shared his death. So, just as Christ was raised from the dead by the wonderful power of the Father, we also can live a new life.

Romans 6:4 NCV

When you invite Christ to rule over your heart, you avail yourself of His power. And make no mistake about it: You and Christ, working together, can do miraculous things. In fact, miraculous things are exactly what Christ intends for you to do, but He won't force you to do great things on His behalf. The decision to become a full-fledged participant in His power is a decision that you must make for yourself.

The words of John 14:12 make this promise: when you put absolute faith in Christ, you can share in His power. Today, trust the Savior's promise and expect a miracle in His name.

The God who spoke still speaks. He comes into our world. He comes into your world. He comes to do what you can't.

Max Lucado

CONFIDENT CHRISTIANITY

You are my hope; O Lord GOD, You are my confidence . . . .

Psalm 71:5 NASB

Jesus has won the victory, so all Christians should live courageously, including you. If you have been touched by the transforming hand of God's Son, then you have every reason to be confident about your future here on earth and your future in heaven. But even if you are a faithful believer, you may find yourself discouraged by the inevitable disappointments and tragedies that are the inevitable price of life here on earth.

If your courage is being tested today, lean upon God's promises. Trust His Son. Remember that God is always near and that He is your protector and your deliverer. When you are worried, anxious, or afraid, call upon Him and accept the touch of His comforting hand. Remember that God rules both mountaintops and valleys—with limitless wisdom and love—now and forever.

If we indulge in any confidence that is not grounded on the Rock of Ages, our confidence is worse than a dream, it will fall on us and cover us with its ruins, causing sorrow and confusion.

C. H. Spurgeon

CONTENTED IN HIM

The Lord *gives strength to his people; the* Lord *blesses his people with peace.*

Psalm 29:11 NIV

Everywhere we turn, or so it seems, the world promises us contentment and happiness. But the contentment that the world offers is fleeting and incomplete. Thankfully, the contentment that God offers is all encompassing and everlasting.

Happiness depends less upon our circumstances than upon our thoughts. When we turn our thoughts to God, to His gifts, and to His glorious creation, we experience the joy that God intends for His children. But, when we focus on the negative aspects of life—or when we disobey God's commandments—we cause ourselves needless suffering.

Do you sincerely want to be a contented Christian? Then set your mind and your heart upon God's love and His grace. Seek first the salvation that is available through a personal relationship with Jesus Christ, and then claim the joy, the contentment, and the spiritual abundance that the Shepherd offers His sheep.

BEYOND THE DIFFICULTIES

It will be hard when all these things happen to you. But after that you will come back to the Lord your God and obey him, because the Lord your God is a merciful God. He will not leave you or destroy you. He will not forget the Agreement with your ancestors, which he swore to them.

Deuteronomy 4:30-31 NCV

Throughout the seasons of life, we must all endure life-altering personal losses that leave us breathless. When we do, God stands ready to protect us. Psalm 147 promises, "He heals the brokenhearted, and binds their wounds" (v. 3 NASB). And God keeps His promises.

Life is often challenging, but as Christians, we must trust the promises of our Heavenly Father. God loves us, and He will protect us. In times of hardship, He will comfort us; in times of sorrow, He will dry our tears. When we are troubled, or weak, or sorrowful, God is with us. His love endures, not only for today, but also for all of eternity.

Whatever hallway you're in—no matter how long, how dark, or how scary—God is right there with you.

Bill Hybels

TEACHING DISCIPLINE

Whoever accepts correction is on the way to life, but whoever ignores correction will lead others away from life.

Proverbs 10:17 NCV

Are you a self-disciplined man? If so, congratulations . . . if not, God wants to have a little talk with you.

You live in a world in which leisure is glorified and indifference is often glamorized. But God has other plans. He did not create you to be ordinary; He created you for far greater things.

Life's greatest rewards aren't likely to fall into your lap. To the contrary, your greatest accomplishments will probably require lots of work, which is perfectly fine with God. After all, He knows that you're up to the task, and He has big plans for you. God will do His part to fulfill those plans, and the rest, of course, is up to you.

Now, are you steadfast in your determination to be a self-disciplined man? If so, congratulations . . . if not, reread this little essay—and keep reading it—until God's message finally sinks in.

CELEBRATING OTHERS

So encourage each other and give each other strength, just as you are doing now.

1 Thessalonians 5:11 NCV

Do you delight in the victories of others? You should. Each day provides countless opportunities to encourage others and to praise their good works. When you do so, you not only spread seeds of joy and happiness, you also obey the commandments of God's Holy Word.

As Christians, we are called upon to spread the Good News of Christ, and we are also called to spread a message of encouragement and hope to the world.

Today, let us be cheerful Christians with smiles on our faces and encouraging words on our lips. By blessing others, we also bless ourselves, and, at the same time, we do honor to the One who gave His life for us.

You can't light another's path without casting light on your own.

John Maxwell

How many people stop because so few say, "Go!"

Charles Swindoll

BECOMING WISE

He who walks with the wise grows wise . . . .

Proverbs 13:20 NIV

Wisdom does not spring up overnight—it takes time. To become wise, we must seek God's wisdom and live according to His Word. And, we must not only learn the lessons of the Christian life, we must also live by them.

Do you seek to live a life of righteousness and wisdom? If so, you must study the ultimate source of wisdom: the Word of God. You must seek out worthy mentors and listen carefully to their advice. You must associate, day in and day out, with godly men and women. And, you must act in accordance with your beliefs. When you do these things, you will become wise . . . and you will be a blessing to your friends, to your family, and to the world.

The essence of wisdom, from a practical standpoint, is pausing long enough to look at our lives—invitations, opportunities, relationships—from God's perspective. And then acting on it.

Charles Stanley

A FOUNDATION OF HONESTY

The honest person will live in safety, but the dishonest will be caught.

Proverbs 10:9 NCV

Lasting relationships are built upon a foundation of honesty and trust. It has been said on many occasions that honesty is the best policy. For believers, it is far more important to note that honesty is God's policy. And if we are to be servants worthy of our Savior, Jesus Christ, we must be honest and forthright in all our communications with others.

Sometimes, honesty is difficult; sometimes, honesty is painful; sometimes, honesty makes us feel uncomfortable. Despite these temporary feelings of discomfort, we must make honesty the hallmark of all our relationships; otherwise, we invite needless suffering into our own lives and into the lives of those we love.

The commandment of absolute truthfulness is really only another name for the fullness of discipleship.

Dietrich Bonhoeffer

BEYOND WORRY

Blessed is he that trusts in the Lord.

Proverbs 16:20 NIV

Because we are imperfect human beings, we worry. Even though we are Christians who have been given the assurance of salvation—even though we are Christians who have received the promise of God's love and protection—we find ourselves fretting over the countless details of everyday life. Jesus understood our concerns when He spoke the reassuring words found in Matthew 6: "Therefore I tell you, do not worry about your life . . . ."

As you consider the promises of Jesus, remember that God still sits in His heaven and you are His beloved child. Then, perhaps, you will worry a little less and trust God a little more, and that's as it should be because God is trustworthy . . . and you are protected.

Anxiety is not only a pain which we must ask God to assuage but also a weakness we must ask him to pardon—for he's told us to take no care for the morrow.

C. S. *Lewis*

LOVE IS A CHOICE

Beloved, if God so loved us, we also ought to love one another.

1 John 4:11 NASB

Love, like everything else in this wonderful world, begins and ends with God, but the middle part belongs to us. During the brief time that we have here on earth, God has given each of us the opportunity to become a loving person—or not. God has given each of us the opportunity to be kind, to be courteous, to be cooperative, and to be forgiving—or not. God has given each of us the chance to obey the Golden Rule, or to make up our own rules as we go. If we obey God's rules, we're safe, but if we do otherwise, we're headed for trouble and fast.

Here in the real world, the choices that we make have consequences. The decisions that we make and the results of those decisions determine the quality of our relationships. It's as simple as that.

Life without love is empty and meaningless no matter how gifted we are.

Charles Stanley

PATS ON THE BACK

So let us try to do what makes peace and helps one another.

Romans 14:19 NCV

Life is a team sport, and all of us need occasional pats on the back from our teammates. In the book of Ephesians, Paul writes, "Do not let any unwholesome talk come out of your mouths, but only what is helpful for building others up according to their needs, that it may benefit those who listen" (4:29 NIV). Paul reminds us that when we choose our words carefully, we can have a powerful impact on those around us.

Since we don't always know who needs our help, the best strategy is to encourage all the people who cross our paths. So today, be a world-class source of encouragement to everyone you meet. Never has the need been greater.

Make it a rule, and pray to God to help you to keep it, never to lie down at night without being able to say: "I have made at least one human being a little wiser, a little happier, or a little better this day."

Charles Kingsley

ENTHUSIASTIC SERVICE

Do your work with enthusiasm. Work as if you were serving the Lord, not as if you were serving only men and women.

Ephesians 6:7 NCV

Do you see each day as a glorious opportunity to serve God and to do His will? Are you enthused about life, or do you struggle through each day giving scarcely a thought to God's blessings? Are you constantly praising God for His gifts, and are you sharing His Good News with the world? And are you excited about the possibilities for service that God has placed before you, whether at home, at work, at church, or at school? You should be.

You are the recipient of Christ's sacrificial love. Accept it enthusiastically and share it fervently. Jesus deserves your enthusiasm; the world deserves it; and you deserve the experience of sharing it.

One of the great needs in the church today is for every Christian to become enthusiastic about his faith in Jesus Christ.

Billy Graham

STANDING UP FOR YOUR FAITH

Be on the alert, stand firm in the faith, act like men, be strong.

1 Corinthians 16:13 NASB

Are you a man whose faith is obvious to your family and to the world, or are you a spiritual shrinking violet? God needs more men who are willing to stand up and be counted for Him.

Genuine faith is never meant to be locked up in the heart of a believer; to the contrary, it is meant to be shared. And a man who wishes to share God's Good News with the world should begin by sharing that message with his own family.

Through every triumph and tragedy, God will stand by your side and strengthen you . . . if you have faith in Him. Jesus taught His disciples that if they had faith, they could move mountains. You can too, and so can your family . . . if you have faith.

Faith means you want God and want to want nothing else.

Brennan Manning

GOD'S PLAN FOR YOUR FAMILY

Unless the LORD builds a house, its builders labor over it in vain; unless the LORD watches over a city, the watchman stays alert in vain.

Psalm 127:1 HCSB

As you consider God's purpose for your own life, you must also consider how your plans will affect the most important people that God has entrusted to your care: your loved ones.

A loving family is a treasure from God. If you happen to be a member of a close-knit, supportive clan, offer a word of thanks to your Creator. He has blessed you with one of His most precious earthly possessions. Your obligation, in response to God's gift, is to treat your family in ways that are consistent with His commandments. So, as you prayerfully seek God's direction, remember that He has important plans for your home life as well as for your professional life. It's up to you to act—and to plan—accordingly.

Calm and peaceful, the home should be the one place where people are certain they will be welcomed, received, protected, and loved.

Ed Young

A PEACE YOU CANNOT BUY

Peace, peace to you, and peace to your helpers! For your God helps you.

1 Chronicles 12:18 NKJV

Sometimes, our financial struggles are simply manifestations of the inner conflict that we feel when we stray from God's path. The beautiful words of John 14:27 remind us that Jesus offers us peace, not as the world gives, but as He alone gives. Our challenge is to accept Christ's peace into our hearts and then, as best we can, to share His peace with our families and friends.

When we summon the courage and the determination to implement a sensible financial plan, we invite peace into our lives. But, we should never confuse earthly peace (with a small "p") with spiritual Peace (the heavenly Peace—with a capital "P"—that flows from the Prince of Peace).

Financial peace can, and should, be yours. But the spiritual peace that stems from your personal relationship with Jesus must be yours if you are to receive the eternal abundance of our Lord. Claim that abundance today.

FRIENDS AND FAMILY

As iron sharpens iron, a friend sharpens a friend.

Proverbs 27:17 NLT

A loving family is a treasure from God; so is a trustworthy friend. If you are a member of a close knit, supportive family, offer a word of thanks to your Creator. And if you have a close circle of trustworthy friends, consider yourself richly blessed.

Today, let us praise God for our family and for our friends. God has placed these people along our paths. Let us love them and care for them. And, let us give thanks to the Father for all the people who enrich our lives. These people are, in a very real sense, gifts from God; we should treat them as such.

It is a reverent thing to see an ancient castle or building not in decay, or to see a fair timber tree sound and perfect. How much more beautiful it is to behold an ancient and noble family that has stood against the waves and weathers of time.

Francis Bacon

THE SEEDS OF GENEROSITY

Freely you have received, freely give.

Matthew 10:8 NIV

Paul reminds us that when we sow the seeds of generosity, we reap bountiful rewards in accordance with God's plan for our lives. Thus, we are instructed to give cheerfully and without reservation: "But this I say, He which soweth sparingly shall reap also sparingly; and he which soweth bountifully shall reap also bountifully. Every man according as he purposeth in his heart, so let him give; not grudgingly, or of necessity: for God loveth a cheerful giver" (2 Corinthians 9:6-7 KJV).

Today, make this pledge and keep it: Be a cheerful, generous, courageous giver. The world needs your help, and you need the spiritual rewards that will be yours when you give it.

All the blessings we enjoy are divine deposits, committed to our trust on this condition: that they should be dispensed for the benefit of our neighbors.

John Calvin

HIS COMFORTING HAND

God, who comforts the downcast, comforted us . . . .

2 Corinthians 7:6 NIV

If you have been touched by the transforming hand of Jesus, then you have every reason to live courageously. Still, even if you are a dedicated Christian, you may find yourself discouraged by the inevitable disappointments and tragedies that occur in the lives of believers and nonbelievers alike.

The next time you find your courage tested to the limit, lean upon God's promises. Trust His Son. Remember that God is always near and that He is your protector and your deliverer. When you are worried, anxious, or afraid, call upon Him and accept the touch of His comforting hand. Remember that God rules both mountaintops and valleys—with limitless wisdom and love—now and forever.

One of the more significant things God will bring out of our grief and depression is an ability to walk constructively with others through theirs. In fact, one of the purposes of God's comfort is to equip us to comfort others.

David B. Biebel

DISCOVERING GOD'S PLANS

It is God who is at work in you, both to will and to work for His good pleasure.

Philippians 2:13 NASB

If you seek to live in accordance with God's will for your life—and you should—then you will live in accordance with His commandments. You will study God's Word, and you will be watchful for His signs. You will associate with fellow Christians who will encourage your spiritual growth, and you will listen to that inner voice that speaks to you in the quiet moments of your daily devotionals.

God intends to use you in wonderful, unexpected ways if you let Him. The decision to seek God's plan and to follow it is yours and yours alone. The consequences of that decision have implications that are both profound and eternal, so choose carefully.

If not a sparrow falls upon the ground without your Father, you have reason to see that the smallest events of your career and your life are arranged by him.

C. H. Spurgeon

EXPECTING THE BEST

This is the day the LORD has made; let us rejoice and be glad in it.

Psalm 118:24 NIV

What do you expect from the day ahead? Are you expecting God to do wonderful things, or are you living beneath a cloud of apprehension and doubt? The familiar words of Psalm 118:24 remind us of a profound yet simple truth: "This is the day which the LORD hath made; we will rejoice and be glad in it" (KJV).

For Christian believers, every day begins and ends with God's Son and God's promises. When we accept Christ into our hearts, God promises us the opportunity for earthly peace and spiritual abundance. But more importantly, God promises us the priceless gift of eternal life.

As we face the inevitable challenges of life here on earth, we must arm ourselves with the promises of God's Holy Word. When we do, we can expect the best, not only for the day ahead, but also for all eternity.

The stars may fall, but God's promises will stand and be fulfilled.

J. I. Packer

BE SUCH A MAN

Don't be obsessed with getting your own advantage. Forget yourselves long enough to lend a helping hand.

Philippians 2:4 MSG

The noted American theologian Phillips Brooks advised, "Be such a man, and live such a life, that if every man were such as you, and every life a life like yours, this earth would be God's Paradise." One tangible way to make the world a more godly place is to spread kindness wherever we go.

Sometimes, when we feel happy or generous, we find it easy to be kind. Other times, when we are discouraged or tired, we can scarcely summon the energy to utter a single kind word. But, God's commandment is clear: He intends that we make the conscious choice to treat others with kindness and respect, no matter our circumstances, no matter our emotions.

Today, as you consider all the things that Christ has done in your life, honor Him by following His commandment and obeying the Golden Rule. He expects no less, and He deserves no less.

NEIGHBORS IN NEED

Each one of us needs to look after the good of the people around us, asking ourselves, "How can I help?" That's exactly what Jesus did.

Romans 15:2-3 MSG

Neighbors. We know that we are instructed to love them, and yet there's so little time . . . and we're so busy. No matter. As Christians, we are commanded by our Lord and Savior Jesus Christ to love our neighbors just as we love ourselves. Period.

This very day, you will encounter someone who needs a word of encouragement or a pat on the back or a helping hand or a heartfelt prayer. And, if you don't reach out to your friend, who will? If you don't take the time to understand the needs of your neighbors, who will? If you don't love your brothers and sisters, who will? So, today, look for a neighbor in need . . . and then do something to help. Father's orders.

There are only two duties required of us—the love of God and the love of our neighbor, and the surest sign of discovering whether we observe these duties is the love of our neighbor.

St. Teresa of Avila

A LIFE OF INTEGRITY

People with integrity have firm footing, but those who follow crooked paths will slip and fall.

Proverbs 10:9 NLT

Charles Swindoll correctly observed, "Nothing speaks louder or more powerfully than a life of integrity." Godly men and women agree.

Integrity is built slowly over a lifetime. It is a precious thing—difficult to build but easy to tear down. As believers in Christ, we must seek to live each day with discipline, honesty, and faith. When we do, at least two things happen: integrity becomes a habit, and God blesses us because of our obedience to Him.

Living a life of integrity isn't always the easiest way, but it is always the right way. And God clearly intends that it should be our way, too.

The man who cannot believe in himself cannot believe in anything else. The basis of all integrity and character is whatever faith we have in our own integrity.

Roy L. Smith

SO LAUGH!

A happy heart makes the face cheerful . . . .

Proverbs 15:13 NIV

Laughter is a gift from God, a gift that He intends for us to use. Yet sometimes, because of the inevitable stresses of everyday living, we fail to find the fun in life. When we allow life's inevitable disappointments to cast a pall over our lives and our souls, we do a profound disservice to ourselves and to our loved ones.

As Christians we have every reason to be cheerful and to be thankful. Our blessings from God are beyond measure, starting, of course, with a gift that is ours for the asking, God's gift of salvation through Christ Jesus.

Few things in life are more absurd than the sight of a grumpy, sour-faced Christian. So today, as you go about your daily activities, approach life with a smile and a chuckle. After all, God created laughter for a reason . . . and Father indeed knows best. So laugh!

Life goes on. Keep on smiling and the whole world smiles with you.

Dennis Swanberg

MENTORS THAT MATTER

The lips of the righteous feed many.

Proverbs 10:21 HCSB

Do you wish to become wise? Then you must walk with people who, by their words and their presence, make you wiser. And, to the best of your ability, you must avoid those people who encourage you to think foolish thoughts or do foolish things.

Today, as a gift to yourself, select, from your friends and family members, a mentor whose judgment you trust. Then listen carefully to your mentor's advice and be willing to accept that advice, even if accepting it requires effort, or pain, or both. Consider your mentor to be God's gift to you. Thank God for that gift, and use it.

The effective mentor strives to help a man or woman discover what they can be in Christ and then holds them accountable to become that person.

Howard Hendricks

BLESSED OBEDIENCE

When you and your children return to the LORD your God and obey him with all your heart and with all your soul according to everything I command you today, then the LORD your God will restore your fortunes and have compassion on you and gather you again from all the nations where he scattered you.

Deuteronomy 30:2-3 NIV

We live in a world filled with temptations, distractions, and countless opportunities to disobey God. But as men who seek to be godly role models for our families, we must turn our thoughts and our hearts away from the evils of this world. We must turn instead to God.

Talking about God is easy; living by His laws is considerably harder. But unless we are willing to live obediently, all our righteous words ring hollow.

How can we best proclaim our love for the Lord? By obeying Him. We must seek God's counsel and trust the counsel He gives. And, when we invite God into our hearts and live according to His commandments, we are blessed today, and tomorrow, and forever.

THE POWER OF PERSEVERANCE

I do not consider myself yet to have taken hold of it. But one thing I do: Forgetting what is behind and straining toward what is ahead, I press on toward the goal to win the prize for which God has called me heavenward in Christ Jesus.

Philippians 3:13-14 NIV

A well-lived life calls for preparation, determination, and, of course, lots of perseverance. As an example of perfect perseverance, we Christians need look no further than our Savior, Jesus Christ. Jesus finished what He began. Despite His suffering, despite the shame of the cross, Jesus was steadfast in His faithfulness to God. We, too, must remain faithful, especially during times of hardship. Sometimes, God may answer our prayers with silence, and when He does, we must patiently persevere.

Are you facing a tough situation? If so, remember this: whatever your problem, God can handle it. Your job is to keep persevering until He does.

Jesus taught that perseverance is the essential element in prayer.

E. M. Bounds

DOING IT NOW

We can't afford to waste a minute, must not squander these precious daylight hours in frivolity and indulgence . . . . Don't loiter and linger, waiting until the very last minute. Dress yourselves in Christ, and be up and about!

Romans 13:13-14 MSG

The habit of procrastination takes a two-fold toll on its victims. First, important work goes unfinished; second (and more importantly), valuable energy is wasted in the process of putting off the things that remain undone. Procrastination results from an individual's short-sighted attempt to postpone temporary discomfort. What results is a senseless cycle of 1. delay, followed by 2. worry followed by 3. a panicky and often futile attempt to "catch up." Procrastination is, at its core, a struggle against oneself; the only antidote is action.

Once you acquire the habit of doing what needs to be done when it needs to be done, you will avoid untold trouble, worry, and stress. So learn to defeat procrastination by paying less attention to your fears and more attention to your responsibilities. God has created a world that punishes procrastinators and rewards men who "do it now."

THE SIMPLE LIFE

Whoever becomes simple and elemental again, like this child, will rank high in God's kingdom.

Matthew 18:4 MSG

You live in a world where simplicity is in short supply. Think for a moment about the complexity of your everyday life and compare it to the lives of your ancestors. Certainly, you are the beneficiary of many technological innovations, but those innovations have a price: in all likelihood, your world is highly complex.

Unless you take firm control of your time and your life, you may be overwhelmed by an ever-increasing tidal wave of complexity that threatens your happiness. But your Heavenly Father understands the joy of living simply, and so should you. So do yourself a favor: keep your life as simple as possible. Simplicity is, indeed, genius. By simplifying your life, you are destined to improve it.

Prescription for a happier and healthier life: resolve to slow down your pace; learn to say no gracefully; resist the temptation to chase after more pleasure, more hobbies, and more social entanglements.

James Dobson

ACCEPTING GOD'S GIFTS

For God loved the world in this way: He gave His only Son, so that everyone who believes in Him will not perish but have eternal life.

John 3:16 HCSB

God loves you—His love for you is deeper and more profound than you can imagine. God's love for you is so great that He sent His only Son to this earth to die for your sins and to offer you the priceless gift of eternal life.

You must decide whether or not to accept God's gift. Will you ignore it or embrace it? Will you return it or neglect it? Will you invite Christ to dwell in the center of your heart, or will you relegate Him to a position of lesser importance? The decision is yours, and so are the consequences. So choose wisely . . . and choose today.

The most profound essence of my nature is that I am capable of receiving God.

St. Augustine

If you want to reach your potential, you need to add a strong work ethic to your talent.

John Maxwell

LOST IN THE CROWD

The fear of human opinion disables; trusting in God protects you from that.

Proverbs 29:25 MSG

Rick Warren observed, "Those who follow the crowd usually get lost in it." We know these words to be true, but oftentimes we fail to live by them. Instead of trusting God for guidance, we imitate our neighbors and suffer the consequences. Instead of seeking to please our Father in heaven, we strive to please our peers, with decidedly mixed results.

Whom will you try to please today: your God or your associates? Your obligation is most certainly not to neighbors, to friends, or even to family members. Your obligation is to an all-knowing, all-powerful God. You must seek to please Him first and always. No exceptions.

There is nothing that makes more cowards and feeble men that public opinion.

Henry Ward Beecher

Choose the opposition of the whole world rather than offend Jesus.

Thomas à Kempis

FOOLISH PRIDE

When you do things, do not let selfishness or pride be your guide. Instead, be humble and give more honor to others than to yourselves.

Philippians 2:3 NCV

Sometimes our faith is tested more by prosperity than by adversity. Why? Because in times of plenty, we are tempted to stick out our chests and say, "I did that." But nothing could be further from the truth. All of our blessings start and end with God, and whatever "it" is, He did it. And He deserves the credit.

Who are the greatest among us? Are they the proud and the powerful? Hardly. The greatest among us are the humble servants who care less for their own glory and more for God's glory. If we seek greatness in God's eyes, we must forever praise God's good works, not our own.

The Bible never says that God resists a drunkard, a thief, or even a murderer, but he does resist the proud. Every kind of sin can be cleansed and forgiven if we humble ourselves and confess it to the Lord.

Jim Cymbala

SEEKING AND FINDING

Ask, and God will give to you. Search, and you will find. Knock, and the door will open for you. Yes, everyone who asks will receive. Everyone who searches will find. And everyone who knocks will have the door opened.

Matthew 7:7-8 NCV

Where is God? He is everywhere you have ever been and everywhere you will ever go. He is with you night and day; He knows your every thought; He hears your every heartbeat.

Sometimes, in the crush of your daily duties, God may seem far away. Or sometimes, when the disappointments and sorrows of life leave you brokenhearted, God may seem distant, but He is not. When you earnestly seek God, you will find Him because He is here, waiting patiently for you to reach out to Him . . . right here . . . right now.

Don't take anyone else's word for God. Find him for yourself, and then you, too, will know, by the wonderful, warm tug on your heartstrings, that he is there for sure.

Billy Graham

THE WISDOM TO CELEBRATE

A miserable heart means a miserable life; a cheerful heart fills the day with a song.

Proverbs 15:15 MSG

The Christian life is a cause for celebration, but sometimes we don't feel much like celebrating. In fact, when the weight of the world seems to bear down upon our shoulders, celebration may be the last thing on our minds . . . but it shouldn't be. As God's children, we are all blessed beyond measure on good days and bad. This day is a nonrenewable resource—once it's gone, it's gone forever. We should give thanks for this day while using it for the glory of God.

God created you in His own image, and He wants you to experience joy and abundance. But, God will not force His joy upon you; you must claim it for yourself. So today, and every day thereafter, celebrate the life that God has given you. Think optimistically about yourself and your future. Give thanks to the One who has given you everything, and trust in your heart that He wants to give you so much more.

HIS LOVE ENDURES

God blesses the people who patiently endure testing. Afterward they will receive the crown of life that God has promised to those who love him.

James 1:12 NLT

Throughout the seasons of life, we must all endure life-altering personal losses that leave us breathless. When we do, we may be overwhelmed by fear, by doubt, or by both. Thankfully, God has promised that He will never desert us. And God keeps His promises.

Life is often challenging, but as Christians, we must trust the promises of our Heavenly Father. God loves us, and He will protect us. In times of hardship, He will comfort us; in times of sorrow, He will dry our tears. When we are troubled or weak or sorrowful, God is with us. His love endures, not only for today, but also for all of eternity.

Teach us to set our hopes on heaven, to hold firmly to the promise of eternal life, so that we can withstand the struggles and storms of this world.

Max Lucado

ACCEPTING HIS GIFTS

You fathers—if your children ask for a fish, do you give them a snake instead? Or if they ask for an egg, do you give them a scorpion? Of course not! If you sinful people know how to give good gifts to your children, how much more will your heavenly Father give the Holy Spirit to those who ask him.

Luke 11:11-13 NLT

God has so much to offer us . . . and He wants us to have the best He has to give—but sometimes, we're simply unwilling or unable to accept the blessings that God wants us to receive. Why? Because we fail to trust God completely, and because we are, at times, surprisingly stubborn.

Are you asking God to move mountains in your life, or are you expecting Him to help you stumble over a few anthills? Whatever the size of your challenges, God is big enough to handle them. Ask for His wisdom and His guidance today, with faith and with fervor, and then watch in amazement as your mountains begin to move.

We honor God by asking for great things when they are a part of His promise. We dishonor Him and cheat ourselves when we ask for molehills where He has promised mountains.

Vance Havner

BEHAVIOR THAT IS CONSISTENT WITH YOUR BELIEFS

If the way you live isn't consistent with what you believe, then it's wrong.

Romans 14:23 MSG

In describing our beliefs, our actions are far better descriptors than our words. Yet far too many of us spend more energy talking about our beliefs than living by them—with predictably poor results.

As believers, we must beware: Our actions should always give credence to the changes that Christ can make in the lives of those who walk with Him.

Your beliefs shape your values, and your values shape your life. Is your life a clearly-crafted picture book of your creed? Are your actions always consistent with your beliefs? Are you willing to practice the philosophies that you preach? Hopefully so; otherwise, you'll be tormented by inconsistencies between your beliefs and your behaviors.

Believe and do what God says. The life-changing consequences will be limitless, and the results will be confidence and peace of mind.

Franklin Graham

A NEW YOU

You have been born again, and this new life did not come from something that dies, but from something that cannot die. You were born again through God's living message that continues forever.

1 Peter 1:23 NCV

Why did Christ die on the cross? Christ sacrificed His life so that we might be born again. This gift, freely given from God's only begotten Son, is the priceless possession of everyone who accepts Him as Lord and Savior.

Let us claim Christ's gift today. Let us walk with the Savior, let us love Him, let us praise Him, and let us share His message of salvation with all those who cross our paths.

The comforting words of Ephesians 2:8 make God's promise clear: "For by grace you have been saved through faith, and that not of yourselves; it is the gift of God" (NKJV). Thus, we are saved not because of our good deeds but because of our faith in Christ. May we, who have been given so much, praise our Savior for the gift of salvation, and may we share the joyous news of our Master's limitless love with our families, with our friends, and with the world.

CONDUCT AND CHARACTER

Lead a quiet and peaceable life in all godliness and honesty.

1 Timothy 2:2 KJV

The Bible makes it clear that God rewards integrity just as surely as He punishes duplicity. So, if we seek to earn the kind of lasting rewards that God bestows upon those obey His commandments, we must make honesty the hallmark of our dealings with others.

Character is built slowly over a lifetime. Character is the sum of every right decision, every honest word, every noble thought, and every heartfelt prayer. It is built upon a foundation of industry, generosity, and humility. Character is a precious thing—difficult to build but easy to tear down. As believers in Christ, we must seek to live each day with discipline, honesty, and faith. When we do, integrity becomes a habit. And God smiles.

People should think less about what they ought to do, and more about what they ought to be. If only their living were good, their work would shine forth brightly.

Meister Eckhart

A RELATIONSHIP THAT HONORS GOD

I am always praising you; all day long I honor you.

Psalm 71:8 NCV

As you think about the nature of your relationship with God, remember this: you will always have some type of relationship with Him—it is inevitable that your life must be lived in relationship to God. The question is not if you will have a relationship with Him; the burning question is whether or not that relationship will be one that seeks to honor Him . . . or not.

Are you willing to place God first in your life? And, are you willing to welcome God's Son into your heart? Unless you can honestly answer these questions with a resounding yes, then your relationship with God isn't what it could be or should be. Thankfully, God is always available, He's always ready to forgive, and He's waiting to hear from you now.

God shows unbridled delight when He sees people acting in ways that honor Him: when He receives worship, when He sees faith demonstrated in the most trying of circumstances, and when He sees tender love shared among His people.

Bill Hybels

HIS TRANSFORMING POWER

Your old life is dead. Your new life, which is your real life—even though invisible to spectators—is with Christ in God. He is your life.

Colossians 3:3 MSG

God's hand has the power to transform your day and your life. Your task is to accept Christ's grace with a humble, thankful heart as you receive the "new life" that can be yours through Him.

Righteous believers who fashion their days around Jesus see the world differently; they act differently, and they feel differently about themselves and their neighbors. Hopefully, you, too, will be such a believer.

Do you desire to improve some aspect of your life? If so, don't expect changing circumstances to miraculously transform you into the person you want to become. Transformation starts with God, and it starts in the quiet corners of a willing human heart—like yours.

Believe and do what God says. The life-changing consequences will be limitless, and the results will be confidence and peace of mind.

Franklin Graham